228 Days Trapped in Paradise

228 Days
Trapped
in Paradise

The diary of an
Expat Chica in Costa Rica

**#1 International Best Selling Author
Nikki Page**

Table of Contents

Foreword:

My husband and I live in Guanacaste, Costa Rica where the weather is always warm, the sun is almost always out and the tropical beaches are beautiful. It's a wonderful place to live. I recommend it! But it's not without the challenges of learning to navigate a different culture and language. As empty nesters and "advanced in years" it's been a fun challenge and adventure to try something new and different. We were prepared for learning a new language, eating new foods, not being able to purchase certain items we were used to, and even driving on roads we wouldn't dream of in the states. But nothing prepared us for March 2020, the start of the global pandemic.

I remember reading the news that borders would be closed. At the time, we didn't know for how long, what it all meant or when we might be able to get back to see our loved ones. I remember when we made the decision to move to Costa Rica. Our families were not all supportive; it's far away! How will you get back if we need you? I remember telling our family; Costa Rica is just a plane flight away, even easier than flying across the US! We certainly didn't anticipate a global pandemic that would lockdown people and countries for months!

One thing I've realized about living in another country is how hard it is to communicate to the people I love the reality of my day to day living. The questions they ask are often quite humorous. They think we essentially live outdoors on the beach sitting in a hammock every day. Though I might be outside and at the beach daily, our house has all the comforts of home – air conditioning, an oven to cook a big turkey, TV's and it's even a smart home complete with high-speed internet and security cameras. I've often thought I should journal my experiences so they could see what it's really like. Then the pandemic hit, and as I shared my experience with friends in other parts of the world, I wished I had been even more diligent about capturing my thoughts, feelings, and experience.

Thanks to my friends and fellow expats – Steve and Nikki Page, I didn't need to write one! They did it for me! 228 Days Trapped in Costa Rica is an excellent read that accurately and poignantly reveals the day to day realities of navigating a pandemic in a developing country. With humor and emotion, they give you a glimpse into the real fear, anxiety, complexity, and even beauty they experienced during their pandemic lockdown.

Only history will judge the decisions and actions of government regulations and decisions, but this book will forever paint the unfolding events as they happened; capturing their raw emotions and perspectives. As you read it, it may remind you of your own experience during this uncertain time and hopefully give you an opportunity to reflect on what you learned during your own 228 days.

Mindy Stoms
United States Expat and Costa Rica Resident

XIV

228 Days Trapped in Paradise

The Diary of an Expat Chica in Costa Rica

Trapped in paradise, it sounds like a dream come true, or is it?

Things you need to know!

I'm going to "Cut The Crap" and talk about how the Coronavirus has affected my life as an expat. The Coronavirus, also known as COVID-19 the Pandemic of 2020 has rolled over to 2021.

It has sent not only me but many others on the emotional roller coaster of anxiety. As a result, many are running back to their home countries. Writing these words makes my heart break, reminding myself this is not the end of the world, but this is no joke. What it takes to travel and live globally as an expat or nomad will never be the same again, and some people are losing everything.

MARCH 2020

Drastic Change Over the Last Couple Months
March 15, 2020

My husband Steve is in California on holiday with his dad and grandfather. He has been stateside for over a month. Our seventeen-year-old daughter, Taya, and I stayed behind at our home in Costa Rica. This was just a normal trip home to see friends and family. Due to the state of emergency caused by COVID, this trip has turned out to be a much different trip than originally planned.

As the numbers continue to grow and panic starts to set in, we start comparing the differences between the two countries. Our video conversations once full of our fun adventures apart have taken a drastic change over the last few weeks.

Instead of, "How was your day at the beach?" or "What new sights did you see?" the conversation sounds more like: "Do your store shelves have food? How's your toilet paper supply? What if we get sick? Is Costa Rica or the USA going to have better care? How are we going to be able to provide? Where are we going to spend the lock-down? Do we want to risk traveling or risk being apart for months?"

There is a huge contrast between Costa Rica and the United States. The reports I am receiving from the U.S. are devastating. Steve and other family members say there is little to no food on some store shelves. Personal hygiene and cleaning products have also been wiped out. If you could find a roll of toilet paper it is like striking gold. People are hoarding food, disinfectant spray, cleaners, pharmaceuticals, and toilet paper among other items for fear of not having it when needed.

On the other hand, stores here in Costa Rica are just the opposite. Shelves are full of food, cleaning products, and personal hygiene. Some stores have started putting up signs that limit certain items to three per household "3 artículos por hoga". Currently, no one seems to be hoarding any of these products.

Costa Rica is Infected & Borders are Closing

Today's phone conversation is about the same, however, the President of Costa Rica is expected to speak in 10 minutes with an update cutting this conversation a little short. Little did I know my expat world was about to change in a matter of minutes.

Listening to President Carlos Alvarado in Spanish, praying I'm not understanding correctly (it's been known to happen; He's speaking in Spanish, and we all know my Spanish sucks). This is one of those times this chica is hoping she's wrong. Waiting for my translator to double-check

before freaking out too much more, it took only a matter of minutes to confirm that my Spanish might not suck as much as some may think, and I understood correctly.

The first confirmed case was tweeted on March 6, 2020, but now the spread is increasing and reaching more areas. Costa Rica is now infected and has "forty-one confirmed cases of COVID-19", Health Minister Daniel Salas said.

It was just a matter of time, and today is the day. Like so many other countries around the world, borders are closing. Starting on Wednesday, March 18, 2020, at 11:59 p.m. no one will be able to enter unless they are a Costa Rica citizen or have special government permission. The borders are scheduled to reopen in 24 days on April 12, 2020.

My visa expires on April 2, 2020. Due to the state of emergency, the government has extended the visa. The President has declared, "Tourists visa (non-Residents) who entered the country after December 17, 2019, may legally remain in Costa Rica until May 17, 2020". (Harris et al.)

Costa Rica vs USA: Where to Ride This out

Our home in Costa Rica is outside a small village. My husband Steve and I work online, and our daughter Taya

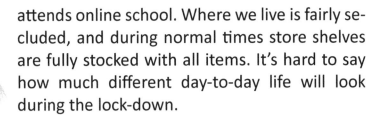

attends online school. Where we live is fairly secluded, and during normal times store shelves are fully stocked with all items. It's hard to say how much different day-to-day life will look during the lock-down.

Medical care in Costa Rica is of good quality, and in my opinion, it's better than in the U.S.
I love my Costa Rican doctors. They saved my life, but that's for another book. Since we live by the beach, it takes about an hour for us to get to a medical care facility. **Medical Manager of the Social Security System (Caja), Mario Ruiz Cubillo** announced on March 10, 2020, that all COVID-19 patients would be treated for free at this time. *(The Tico Times)* Way to go Costa Rica just another reason why this country rocks!

The phone continues to ring as I wait impatiently for Steve to pick up. Ding-ding-ding rings out as the message box on my computer starts blowing up with people asking me what they should do. I find myself feeling overwhelmed, how do I help others when I don't even know what to do at this moment?

My fingers are typing as quickly as they can, looking up flights for Steve to fly this way as quickly as possible. There's only one flight from Sacramento California (SMF), where Steve is, to Liberia, Costa Rica (LIR). This is a red-eye with a couple of seats available and leaves at 12:30 AM on the 17th with a layover in Houston, Texas. If he takes this flight, he should land before the borders are closed and receive a 90-day tourist visa stamp in his U.S.

passport.

To get this flight, he must be at the airport in less than 8 hours. If he chooses not to take this flight he will not be allowed back into the country until the travel ban is lifted. Steve, please answer the phone!

If I can find a flight that hasn't been canceled and still has seats available, Taya and I could fly back to the U.S. immediately. Last I checked, these seats would cost about $1200 each, and that's about $930 more than what we normally pay for a ticket! I need two of them, so it will cost $2400! Plus, there's a high probability of the flight being canceled. We also would have to leave the dogs because there is no time to do paperwork.

Expat Roulette

Feeling like I'm playing a game of "Expat Roulette", the stakes are higher than ever. In addition to our personal lives, flying can have far-reaching effects. If we come in contact with someone infected, we could help spread the virus. We are not making these decisions lightly. Life-changing choices must be made in a matter of minutes. Two phone calls and no answer yet. Damn it, Steve pick up the phone!

Pressed for a Decision

Finally, he answers, and my voice rings out over the phone.

"Steve, we have to make a decision, or we will be separated for the foreseeable future!"

"Oh Babe," he could hear I was about ready to have a breakdown as the words came across the receiver.

"I told you they were going to close the borders and there is only one flight left! You need to get on it if you want to come back!!!"

"Do you really think they will open in 24 days?"

"No, I have been following the numbers, talking to the doctors in both countries and even in the private travel groups, people are saying October some are even predicting 2021! Maybe they are all just freaking out."

"What about the risk of me traveling back to Colorado with my MS and lung problems? Not only for me, but all our family members have been isolating together. Where will we go since we can't risk going home?"

We go back and forth with questions and best guesses for an eternity. In actuality it was only about 10 minutes. Based on the numbers, doctor's recommendations, and other research the decision has been made.

Escaping the U.S. Pandemic 2020
Steve's Perspective

It sounds so dramatic, "Escaping the U.S. Pandemic". But that is my reality. I have spent the past couple of months visiting family in the United States. When I left Costa Rica at the beginning of February, there was very little talk about the disease that was erupting in China.

At that time, a one-way ticket was booked because I wasn't sure about my exact return date. I was planning on staying until late March.

After visiting the majority of my family in Colorado, I took a flight to Sacramento, California to visit my 90-year-old grandfather. The idea was to spend some time helping him while my aunt, who is his caregiver, went on a trip to Israel.

California, Israel, a Quarantine, and Bare Shelves

About a week before flying to California, my aunt called to let us know that their trip might be canceled due to the epidemic. They wouldn't know for sure if the trip was happening until up to the day it was scheduled. My father and I decided to continue our plans to visit my grandfather regardless of their trip.

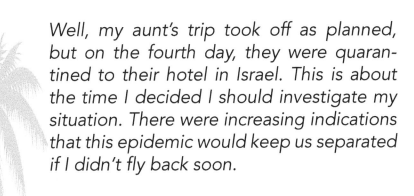

Well, my aunt's trip took off as planned, but on the fourth day, they were quarantined to their hotel in Israel. This is about the time I decided I should investigate my situation. There were increasing indications that this epidemic would keep us separated if I didn't fly back soon.

It is Clear That People in the States are

Starting to React to the Impending Threat

While caring for my grandpa, we made a few grocery runs. The United States had told people to keep social distancing in crowds, but things were fairly normal. The difference was spotted when we went to the store.

None of the stores we visited had hand sanitizer or cleaning wipes. Two of the three stores we went to had no toilet paper. The third had toilet paper but much of the food was picked over and some shelves were bare. The toilet paper was limited to two small packages per person.

Catching the Last Flight
2:00 p.m. March 16th

It is time. After sorting through the most recent information, I am escaping the U.S. Pandemic. Most flights to Costa Rica have been canceled. Jumping on the United.com website, I booked the last flight from Sacramento that will arrive before the border closure.

Shout out to United who allowed the flight change at no additional fee. Flight leaves in 10 hours, meaning I have to be at the airport in 8 hours to depart Sacramento International Airport (SMF) just past midnight. There will be a layover in Houston at 6 a.m. and I will land in Liberia, Costa Rica (LIR) at noon.

I'm spending my final few hours before my flight watching an old John Wayne movie with my grandfather, packing bags, and prepare to say goodbyes. My dad drops me at the departure doors of the airport at exactly 10 p.m. and I'm off.

Quiet Airports & Empty Flights

The Sacramento Airport is quiet. There are fewer travelers than usual. It's not quite a ghost town, but not many people are in the terminal or at the gate. Check-in and security are short lines and very quick. I get to my gate with plenty of time to wait.

Upon locating my seat, I break out the disinfectant wipes and hand sanitizer. Wiping down the seat in front of me and all around, not knowing if I'm being overly cautious or just careful, but with this one, I'd rather err on the side of caution.

This first flight is very empty. There are only about 30 people on it. I am able to sit in the window seat and the nearest person is on the opposite window. It feels a bit eerie that the plane is this vacant.

Feeling like Tom Hanks in "The Terminal"

When I arrive in Houston, the people get even more sparse. Making my way to the gate, I find a chair near an outlet to relax, settling in for the three-hour layover. Fifteen minutes past six in the morning is not exactly rush hour, but normally this airport terminal and the bar serving breakfast would be buzzing. This morning it is just me and the flight crew waiting to head to the tropics.

Escaping

So, this is it. This next flight takes me out of my home country for the foreseeable future. I'm betting on Costa Rica as my sanctuary. I feel a bit nervous but trust we have made the best possible choice with the information available.

The flight to Liberia is bare-bones, making it feel like it's a chartered flight. Without bending my head around the seats, I cannot see another passenger. I'm conflicted between enjoying the empty flight and the implications of why it is empty and praying I have chosen wisely.

Bienvenido a Costa Rica!

After touch down officially in Costa Rica, I collect my bags and head through customs, where I'm able to walk straight through. At this time, both the United States and Costa Rican governments have been announcing 14 days of quarantine. However, I was not given any instruction to quarantine. My passport was stamped and now reads "17 Mar. 2020" with a handwritten 90 on the stamp line which means I'm now legally able to be in Costa Rica until June 15, 2020.

After collecting my bags, I head to the parking lot to meet my ride. But... The girls are not here...

Of course, they are late to pick me up. Why would I expect them to be on time for the apocalypse?

Relieved when they do finally show up that we are reunited. Confident in my decision, I believe it is best for the girls and me to endure the lock-down in Costa Rica. Even though I was not given instruction for the next 14 days, I will be spending my time

away from other people.

(End of Steve's entry)

U.S. Health Advisory
March 19, 2020

"U.S. State Department issued a Global Level 4 Health Advisory," telling its citizens to "avoid all international travel due to the global impact of COVID-19." (ACSSANJOSE)

The world is going to be shut down. I guess if we must stay home, we might as well do it in our vacation home. This rental is really a piece of paradise.

Beaches are Closed
March 20, 2020

Taya and I call the beach down the dirt road our private paradise. It's a public beach; as a matter of fact, by law, all beaches in Costa Rica for the first 50 meters at high tide are public lands. Our beach has great surf with very few people. We spend our mornings on the beach taking the dogs, D.O.G. and Titan, out so we can all get our fresh air and exercise.

Some days we can see a couple of surfers off in the distance. Most mornings we only see a few people. On more than one occasion we have had the entire beach to ourselves. So, the social distancing directives have not had a huge impact on our normal daily lives; however, some things have changed.

Today Costa Rica announces all beaches are to be closed. The police came and put-up roadblocks removing access to the Marbella beach.

The reason for this is that the people from the city who were told not to go to work to minimize the spread of the virus decided it would be a good time to camp on the beaches creating crowds where usually there's no one in sight.

The beaches look more like Semana Santa also known as Holy Week. This occurs the week before and the weekend during Easter. The locals swarm the beaches during their holiday week, so the roadblocks are to help disperse the crowd and ensure no large gatherings. Therefore, all beaches are closed.

Don't get me wrong, I am not complaining, just trying to understand what is going on. However, this is a big change in our daily routine and exercise. As I mentioned before, we visit the beach almost daily and our dogs run and play in the water. Our routine gives us a chance to swim in the ocean while walking the beach and enjoying the fresh air and sunshine.

We get our daily dose of vitamins. An extra dose of vitamin "sea" is always on my list when my Multiple Sclerosis is hurting my muscles. The healing sea waters are powerful if you have never tried them, I highly recommend you do.

Since the government started closing beaches, public spaces, restaurants, bars, parks, land, sea, and air travel we start to ask ourselves what we are going to need to ride this out. The plan is to self-quarantine at our home for the next three to four weeks.

Prohibition 2020
2nd Entry for March 20, 2020

You've got to be kidding me! The news just keeps getting worse. As if the beaches being closed was not enough.

Costa Rica STOPS the sale of alcohol at noon!

Just down at the local store where they informed me the black plastic was to block off the coolers full of liquor. The government is mandating the shops stop selling alcohol today at noon. This is a shocking contrast to what's going on in Colorado as the state continues to allow both alcohol and marijuana sales.

"Los concejos municipales de Guanacaste están prohibiendo la venta de licor en sus cantones por la emergencia del nuevo coronavirus." *(Esquivel)*

Do you have enough beer, wine, and liquor?

Costa Rica's going dry today at noon. Make sure to stock up on guaro so you can make your Naughty Granizado with us.

What is a Naughty Granizado?

Get your Free recipe here
https://theultimatecostarica.com/recipes/naughty-granizado

Things are getting serious NO Alcohol, No Beaches, NO National Parks, and NO Travel. Stay safe everyone!

So, What's new?
March 21, 2020

As the country begins lock-down, I would like to say it's not much different for us. Since we work from home and our daughter attends school online, normal weeks we can go for days without seeing anyone.

However, it is affecting us more than I thought it would in our everyday lives.

Living outside a small village called Marbella with a population of about 300 people. Our closest neighbor is about a block away. The beach is less than a mile and the village has a soccer field with a small school, a couple of small restaurants plus a local watering hole. It reminds me of a little town called Satana, Kansas, where my dad grew up. There are two small mini supers, as well.

A mini super is a small shop that can be part of people's homes, in commercial complexes or small standalone buildings. The further away from tourist areas, the more often they are part of a family's porch rather than their own entity. As in other countries, you pay for the convenience of the location of these shops, so the prices are considerably higher than the larger mercados (markets). Most of the mini supers have eggs, milk, drinks, liquor,

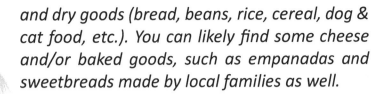

and dry goods (bread, beans, rice, cereal, dog & cat food, etc.). You can likely find some cheese and/or baked goods, such as empanadas and sweetbreads made by local families as well.

Shopping and Being Prepared

The way we eat

We try to buy as much as we can from the local farmers and our mini super stores. Our family eats mostly fresh fruits and vegetables, shelf life is not long. Right now, we only have a week of food on hand. Not knowing how long the social distancing directives will last, this time I find myself putting more of the processed foods that we normally don't eat on the shopping list. These are foods I try my best not to buy. Not only are they unhealthy, but since we cut them out of our daily diets, we all feel so much better.

Maybe it's because I learned so much about nutrition and health when we wrote our cookbook "Cut The Crap Kitchen: How To Cook On A Budget In Costa Rica" or maybe it's just because I know the foods make me feel awful and sluggish. None of us want to see the weight loss that we have experienced come back.

The thought of bringing this kind of food back into the house just makes me want to scream, but I must make sure that my family has food if we can't go to town and the delivery trucks stop coming to the house.

Tip: If you don't have the crap food in your house it can't be eaten. Stop buying it was the first step to healthy eating in our home.

Even though we have two mini supers in town, you never know what they will have in stock or what food will be available. The major super mercados and stores are all about an hour drive away. We try to only make a trip every couple weeks. With the current situation, I must ask myself, "Will the mini supers have anything left in a week?"

How Long Will Supplies Last

My kids in the States have been reporting empty shelves for over two weeks. Toilet paper, cleaning products, or personal hygiene have been nonexistent for even longer. Costa Rica imports most of these products. Keep in mind that both domestic and commercial flights have been stopped; in addition, shipping boats are not allowed to dock. The current state of affairs can have a huge impact on what I'm able to buy in the next few weeks.

Most of these stores don't have stock rooms so, "what you see is what you get". The bread truck that stops by my casa on Mondays also stocks both the stores, but it didn't make deliveries this week. What is a mini super going to look like in a week as the government continues to close more things and deliveries decrease?

After a long debate with Steve, we decided to do our shopping trip a week early. We will leave first thing in the morning - not as early as normal because most stores are allowing the elderly in from 8-9 to protect them from crowds.

Life Goes on

Wrapping up this entry from the comfort of my porch, I'm watching a troop of howler monkeys settling down for the evening in the trees across the way. While the sun sets, I'm listening to the birds singing in the trees and getting ready for another relaxing evening. Except for my husband and daughter, the only people I saw today were the few people in their cars and on their motorcycles as they passed by.

Pretty sure tomorrow will be a lot like today apart from a quick shopping trip. So, what's life like during a pandemic in Costa Rica? From my porch, it doesn't look much different.

Venturing Out
March 22, 2020

So blessed to see a fresh fruit truck on our way to town making sure to buy extra fruits to cut and freeze. Unlike when we were in the states, we don't have a big deep freezer. Our property manager is letting me borrow her dehydrator so I can dehydrate fruits. This is great because I have been thinking about getting one for myself.

Once we arrived in town, we were able to shop at the supermarket and purchase the dry goods we needed such as pasta, coffee, and bread. Choosing to go to a second store called Maxi Pali (it's a chain store owned by Walmart) for better pricing and bigger selection on cleaning products.

Unlike the stores in the United States, people in Costa Rica are not hoarding. All the products and food we need are available and fully stocked. Some products still have signs that read no more than 3 per household "3 artículos por hogar". The government has also announced that there will be no price gouging.

With the supplies loaded up, we began our hour trip back to our remote home in the jungle. All I can say is Taya tries, but she is not a good co-pilot. We are not even out of town, and she is snoring. The only traffic

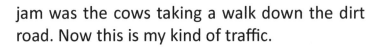

jam was the cows taking a walk down the dirt road. Now this is my kind of traffic.

After getting home I started the dehydrate process. This is my first time and I quickly realize that while my family might love eating the dried-out fruit, it's not worth the work of cutting, and the hours of drying it also heated my whole house. This chica will not be bringing one back in her suitcase next time.

Residency is not all it's Cracked up to be!
March 23, 2020

Costa Rica Expats Think Twice Before Going Home!

If you have Costa Rican residency or are in the process you might want to think twice before leaving! Residency has always been a hot topic in our home since it comes with many benefits like no border runs, health care, and gives you more legal rights. To me this is a big deal when owning homes and business in any country.

With that said, it also comes with some negative impacts as well. It can be expensive to file, the process can take years to complete, and not everyone qualifies. Just like everything, nothing is free. Once you establish residency, you have to pay into the government health care (Caja). Caja is similar to Medicaid in the United States. It's not bad health care, but the system is over run taking months if not years for some treatments. Although paying into Caja is not optional, many still choose to use private doctors and pay out of pocket. We would probably pay out of pocket to use our current doctors and as a result would not get much benefit from it.

Residency is something that I always said we would obtain if we owned property. The thought of not having as many rights as possible before investing a huge amount money is a big deal to me. Only having a tourist

visa and not being able to get to our home or investments has always been a concern. Gaining residency gives you more rights easing this concern. At one point in time, I even had a list of 10 reason why the country would keep us out, Civil unrest was at the top and global pandemic did not even make the list, but at this point it would not matter!

"At 12:54 Monday, March 23, 2020, the President announced that any foreign national that leaves the country during the COVID-19 crisis will lose their status. This applies to any Temporary or Permanent Resident, Special Categories, etc. and people with applications in progress. If you are interested in keeping your Immigration status, please do not depart the country." (Alvarado et al.)

It's going to be interesting to see how all this plays out. At this time Costa Rica is still allowing citizens to come and go. In the upcoming weeks and months, immigrant parents of citizen children (kids born in Costa Rica) were even denied access. The citizen children were allowed in, but not their non-citizen parents. Lawsuits have been filed as human rights and immigration attorneys start to battle the governments over people's rights. Lawsuits like this are not just happening here but in countries around the world.

Driving Restrictions
March 24, 2020

No driving! The government just announced a nation-wide vehicle restriction between the hours of 10 p.m. and 5 a.m. beginning tonight. It's going to be interesting to see how the people around the beach towns handle this. *(Zúñiga)*

In Costa Rica, not being able to drive during certain days and hours of the week is nothing new. Driving restrictions have been implemented on license plates in the major city since before we moved to Costa Rica. However, the restrictions were to slow down the highly congested areas of the city. Not being able to drive around the beach towns is a whole new game.

This should not be too big of a problem for us since we don't drive most days anyways.

Health Alert
March 25, 2020

"Dear God, please help me find peace through all of this!" were the words I cried out today after opening my email.

"Health Alert – U.S. Embassy San Jose (25 March 2020)
Location: Costa Rica – Level 4: Do Not Travel
Event: Due to the Costa Rican ban on non-resident for-eigners entering the country, commercial carriers are slowing and stopping regular flights. As of today, most carriers have suspended service to and from both San Jose and Liberia airports. As far as the Embassy is aware, Delta is the only carrier operating direct flights from San Jose/Liberia and the United States, and we understand they will be suspending daily service as of March 31. Their current plan includes two flights on April 18 and 25, but that is subject to change. Obviously, the situa-tion is fluid and even the scheduled flights could be sus-pended on short notice. We urge all U.S. citizens who wish to depart Costa Rica to do so now. U.S. "(ACSSANJOE)

Let's call it what it is. This shit is about ready to get real. You better buckle up chica; because not being able to get back to your home country for the unforeseeable future is now your reality!

Should I be Masking?
March 26, 2020

Currently, Costa Rica is not requiring us to wear a mask.

It's no secret I have Multiple Sclerosis. This autoimmune disease puts me at a higher risk for illness. My social media as well as pictures on the news show everyone wearing masks. People have taken to social media to show how they are making masks at home from bandannas to homemade masks out of shirts, everyone seems to have one.

We even watched a family video of Grandpa Craig in Colorado showing us before work how to fold a bandanna to make a mask. It was nice to see that the kids even jumped in to show what they were doing. It took only a couple of minutes before Aunt Sandy showed all of us up (in our defense, she's the craft lady).

A quick search on both the (CDC) and (WHO) websites show that they are currently recommending healthy people not mask.

So why is the world masking?

A call to my Dra. last night was very interesting. When I

asked what her thoughts about wearing a mask were, she informed me that I could pick a surgical mask up both at her office or the local pharmacy. If I wanted a good tightly woven cotton mask, there were some at the little store next to the Auto Mercado in Tamarindo, or I could call the lady directly and she would meet me with one. Now that I have been told where I can buy a mask the question still remains, should I be wearing one?

The answer to this question was, "If it makes you feel safer then I would wear one if not don't worry about it just make sure that you wash your hands."

No TV for the Page Household
March 27, 2020

The goal is to stay focused. Just because we are stuck at home doesn't mean it's time to watch TV and be lazy. Steve and I will be working through an online course we are taking as well as spending time writing our next book. Taya will keep meeting with her math tutor as she continues with online school. All of us have downloaded books that we will spend time reading. Throughout the day we will all take a little time to have a meal together for some social time while in isolation.

What are you doing with your time? No Netflix in the Page house. School, writing, and online real estate are all that's happening right now. No one has to leave the house. Learning how to work anywhere was a game-changer for us.

How are You Using Your Time Today?

Now don't get me wrong, taking downtime can be a good thing; however, you need to ask yourself how long you are willing to be still. Rest is one thing but getting comfortable in doing nothing is not a good thing.

Gold
March 29, 2020

How much is toilet paper worth to you?

I'm just going to come out and say it, this chica has a TP obsession! Every bathroom needs to be stocked plus back-up! This has been the case since I moved out on my own when I was eighteen years old. In my defense, it has always been a sign of wealth.

Story From Mommy Hay

Since I was a little girl, I treated toilet paper like gold because of stories my grandma told me during my summer trips to Liberal, Kansas. This amazing woman, who the world referred to as Mommy Hay (short for Hazel), would fill our days and nights with stories from the old days when she was a little girl in the Great Depression. One of the stories was about a little girl and her dream was to have toilet paper in her bathrooms.

As you can imagine, this was very complex for my 6-year-old brain. There was a never-ending supply of toilet paper. As a matter of fact, if you used the last roll, you were expected to replace it with one of the extras rolls from under the sink. I asked her why any little girl would waste her time dreaming about something so pointless.

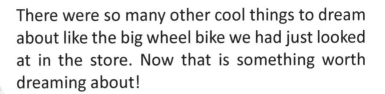

There were so many other cool things to dream about like the big wheel bike we had just looked at in the store. Now that is something worth dreaming about!

She proceeded to tell me how only the wealthy could afford such a luxury and her family was not one of the wealthy. Then she told me that when you must decide between food or an expensive way to wipe your backside, food wins hands down. She went on to tell me other ways she had to save on money like using rags to wipe. The thought of this was just appalling!

I told her there is no way I could ever see any of us doing that! I will never forget her response "we are now the wealthy so consider yourself blessed and stop using so much of my gold (aka TP) in one sitting or tomorrow there might only be rags." But, she told me not to worry because she would show me how to wash the rags without using the washing machine because that appliance was even more of a blessing than TP!

I think back to these stories, and it makes me uneasy. My children and parents report to me that store shelves are empty, and they all are on their last roll of TP. Worried is an understatement! Mommy Hay's stories always came with warnings. "If you see signs of this, you better get prepared as history always repeats itself. A Depression is no fun! You are too soft my child."

My parent's and children's stories sound like Mommy

Hay's, but my story is much different. Every store in Costa Rica is fully stocked. So, the Costa Rica limit of three is not a problem for me. This chica only needs a big pack a month because she has her gold stocked up already. I'm not buying any more than we will use before my next trip to town.

While many people in the U.S. went without toilet paper for weeks, most of my friends have reported installing bidet systems that hook to their toilet to clean their backsides. I even personally witnessed the price gouging of toilet paper on platforms like Amazon. com where I was able to find a listing for a 4 pack for $399.99! As quickly as the listings were put up, the company seemed to pull them down.

As an advertiser, I can confirm that there have been numerous emails sent out warning anyone who is price gouging that they will be banned; but let's face it, this stuff is now gold in the U.S., and people with money are buying it.

I'm kind of an analyst geek- I like to look at the numbers and break things down. So, let's take a look at how much Mommy Hay's gold has grown over the last 30 years.

A quick google search shows the average price of toilet paper in 1980 when I was a kid was $1.09 for 4 pkg of

Charmin. This breaks out to .27 cents a roll. That sounds cheap, but you have to remember that was back in the 80s. I was buying .10 cent candy at the little store down the street from grandma's house. Back then you could buy a new car for around $7,000 and the gas to get around in this new vehicle would cost you about $1.20 a gallon. My parents bought their first 4-bedroom home in Colorado for $71K.

The cost went up about $.10 per roll in the '90s. However, *"For the 52 weeks ended October 4, 2020, the average price per unit of toilet tissue was 7.91 U.S. dollars. This represents an increase of more than 60 cents from 2019 Toilet tissue was the leading household paper product sold in U.S. multi-outlet retail in 2020."* (Gelder).

Supply and demand it's a funny thing. Let's face it, it doesn't matter the price of a good if the good is nowhere to be found. So, I ask you once again how much is a roll of toilet paper worth to you?

I can hear Mommy Hay from the grave, "Your friends were blessed to be able to buy a water system to help them." My response back to her would be, "They are even more blessed to have water since we have been without it for over 24 hours (not because of the end of the world it's just part of life in Costa Rica). Praying it will be turned back on soon, unlike Tamarindo and Langosta (other Costa Rica towns) we have never gone longer than 48 hours without water in Marbella.

Today is July 4, 2021, and I'm doing my final read of this book before handing it off to my editors. I just jumped on to Amazon.com and Walmart to see how much a roll would cost me today, both sites were comparable. In the U.S, I could have it brought right to my front door for no additional cost for .99 cents a roll. This is about the same price I was paying in Costa Rica. We have seen a 380% increase in the price of toilet paper over the last 30 years. All I can say is this chica should have bought some stock in the toilet paper market.

#RIPmommyhay June 10, 1913, to February 4, 2004

APRIL 2020

Mask vs NO Mask - Pick a Side!
April 3, 2020

It's astonishing in just a couple of weeks how quickly the lines were drawn and the fighting over masking started. It has been 11 days since I asked if I should be masking. In order to get into stores and work, my family state side has been masking for almost a month.

I am finding this interesting since doctors, the Center for Disease Control (CDC), and the World Health Organization (WHO) all had said not to mask. But, social media is showing people ways to mask so everyone is following, including the stores and workplaces.

The CDC Announces the Public Should Wear Masks While the WHO is not on the Same Page.

The WHO and CDC took opposing sides on masking today. Let the fighting and confusion begin, from an analyst perspective it has been interesting watching all of this unfold.

The debate about covering a healthy person's face and presuming healthy people are sick until proven otherwise will go down in western world history as a first.

The nasty in people has sure come out on social media.

It's more like being on a playground where all the kids are fighting and picking sides, and this was even before the announcement from the CDC. *(Chavez and Andone)*

Amplifying the confusion, world leaders, doctors, and health organizations seem to not agree at all!

To say the world is confused as to what to do is an understatement!

Now that the two leading health organizations have taken different sides it will be interesting to see how the fighting on the playground today plays out.

Captain Crunch Wrap
April 4, 2020

Those moments you look at your husband and think *"are you kidding me?"*. Today was one of those days as he held the injured bird telling me the neighbor said she would have taken it if he wanted her to. "Why didn't you let her take it?" were my words. He went on to tell me he thought Taya could handle the bird.

This is one of those moments that as a mother I welcome hands-on learning. But let's face it, anytime an animal is involved, especially an injured one, means mom will be picking up some of the slack in taking care of it. I have no clue what to do with an injured bird, but Taya just might.

My girl is amazing. She has spent her free time over the years volunteering at many different animal shelters in Costa Rica. She has assisted in caring for dogs, birds, monkeys, snakes, and even crocodiles. This momma is a little jealous when she shows me pictures of my favorite animals, monkeys. Yep, I'm a sucker for monkeys. Watching her learn how to handle them has been inspiring. She has spent hours chopping food, and cleaning cages, in hopes that the animals heal enough to be released back into the wild or find forever homes.

Taya has also volunteered at an animal shelter called Halfway Home. It's a nonprofit shelter located outside of Villareal. Founded by Dr. Cavallini, Taya has had the privilege of working side by side with the vets over the years. If you are ever looking to adopt a furry pet or a place to volunteer this is the place to go.

Not knowing if the vet was going to answer the phone at six in the morning. I went running to my social media asking what to do as Taya placed her call. Once again, the outpouring of help from others was amazing. Dr. Cavallini picked up the phone immediately, sanctuaries around the country reached out to offer help while others volunteered to help with driving if needed. This was crucial because thanks to restrictions we are not able to drive today. All of this happened within the first 5 minutes of my post.

What a blessing, another opportunity for hands-on learning. As much as I love online school where she is taking vet courses, hands-on learning is priceless.

Now Taya's on a mission with the vets Dr. Cavallini and Dra. Leticia to save the bird who we named Captain Crunch Wrap. I am living in a world like no other as Steve and Taya talk like pirates while building a bird perch for our injured friend, that is currently wrapped up in what was once my favorite bath towels.

What can I say, it was all I had on me literally when Steve yelled up the hill asking for a towel.

I'm just praying this bird doesn't die. The vet called to inform me that he had told Taya the chances of the bird making it through the night was slim, but you never know. We all just have to wait and see.

One thing is for sure, that girl has a heart of gold. Like a new mother who is scared to leave her newborn baby's crib side, Taya spent her night right next to his box. This momma was finally able to convince her to let me take over at two the next morning, so she could get a little sleep before school.

Do I Flee to my Home Country or Stay in a Foreign Country?
April 9, 2020

The U.S. Embassy just informed me United Airlines is offering "ONE FLIGHT HOME". This repatriation flight is for expats and vacationers who have been stranded for weeks in Costa Rica.

> *"Event: IMPORTANT NOTICE REGARDING REPATRIATION FLIGHT TO THE UNITED STATES. PLEASE READ CAREFULLY.*
> *The U.S. Embassy in San Jose and the U.S. State Department have coordinated with United Airlines to offer a commercial flight from Juan Santamaria Airport (SJO) in San Jose, Costa Rica to Houston, Texas (IAH) on Friday, April 17. The flight will depart SJO at 11:30 am and arrive at IAH at 4:30 pm. This flight is open to public booking; you are encouraged to book ASAP as seats are limited."* (Ramirezej | 9 April)

A repatriation flight is one that is initiated by the embassy in coordination with airlines to return citizens to their home country. When the embassy encourages leaving a country, they try to accommodate the citizens by coordinating flights with commercial airlines. Repatriation flights are also used to return illegal immigrants and sol-

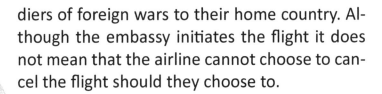

diers of foreign wars to their home country. Although the embassy initiates the flight it does not mean that the airline cannot choose to cancel the flight should they choose to.

This new flight is a way back. It's available, but seating is limited and filling up fast!

According to the United States Embassy, if I don't book this flight, I run the risk of being stuck again. It was one thing not being able to get back into Costa Rica but not being able to get home even on an overpriced flight has been a whole different story. If I book this flight, I will lose the life I've built over the past five years. But I wouldn't be stuck in a foreign country with limited rights, I would be in my home country during this global pandemic. By choosing to take this flight, my Costa Rican Tourist Visa, housing, automobiles, our finances, and healthcare will be directly impacted.

Making the wrong decision, I could end up spreading the virus by encountering someone infected during travels. If I became infected I could spread it to fellow travelers in the airport. It could have a global effect on many countries that have called a state of emergency.

This decision in the next couple of minutes plays into a crazy game of what feels like "Expat Roulette", where contestants must choose between family, health, country, and life. How much do I risk, It's all at stake!

The decision must be made quickly. Like I said, it will have

a direct effect on every aspect of our lives. If I don't book this flight, I run a high risk that it will fill up quickly and I could end up stuck in a foreign country, again holding nothing but a U.S. Passport with an expired 90-day visa stamp that reads "03 ENE 2020" (03 January 2020) meaning I should have left on or before April 2, 2020.

Worst Case Scenario

This was the worst-case scenario I came up with six years ago when telling my parents and children about becoming an expat family. All of them asked, "What if something happens?" and I would answer jokingly, "We can always come home by land, sea, or air. If all three of these are closed at the same time, the world has bigger problems".

"We're talking the end of the world apocalypse scenario like "Walking Dead" and at that point, it won't matter. Even after 9/11, flights came back quickly. So, remember, unless it's the end of the world, I can and always will be able to get back to you." However, this is no joke. The risk of not being able to get home is real.

Days that were once full of words about travel and living out dreams have been replaced with words like:

LEAVE NOW IF YOU WANT TO GO BACK - EXPECT TO STAY INDEFINITELY - FLIGHTS CANCELED - BORDERS CLOSED - BOATS NOT ALLOWED - NUMBER OF PEOPLE SICK HAVE

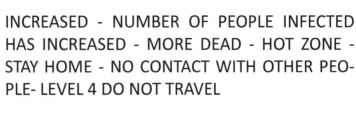

INCREASED - NUMBER OF PEOPLE INFECTED HAS INCREASED - MORE DEAD - HOT ZONE - STAY HOME - NO CONTACT WITH OTHER PEOPLE- LEVEL 4 DO NOT TRAVEL

The messenger inbox and emails that were once full of people asking me for help with vacation and retirement plans are now filled with:

"HELP! How do I get home? What country has more deaths today? Is anyone sick? What airlines are flying, Is there food on the shelves in your country? Do we stay or should we go? Where do we quarantine when we get to our destination?"

I don't know about you, but these words scare the hell out of me!!! They have brought tears to my eyes while keeping me up at night. I hold my breath every time the phone rings, praying there is not an emergency where travel restrictions will keep us from being able to get to loved ones in time.

Do I Stay or Flee?
The signs of the world ending have made it so the next flight might not be for months. Missing my parents and kids, this chica has never been so homesick in her life! This tops my first international trip at age 18 to London when my dad spent hundreds of dollars on a collect call from London to Colorado on New Year's Eve night. What can I say, my dad is my best friend and starting a New Year without him was hard and making the call was priceless.

Knowing that it may be months before I have another opportunity to go stateside, I consider the risks of leaving, but there are pros to staying as well. At this moment we have no shortage of food or personal hygiene products. Steve and I just called our kids and parents who are all on lock-down and fortunately all are healthy now. As of now, we have access to free medical care for COVID-19 if needed plus there is a New COVID hospital in Costa Rica. *(A.M. Costa Rica)*

We have a secluded home and live in a low populated area. Civil unrest is something that is very concerning to me but currently doesn't seem to be a problem. More than anything, the country still feels safe at this moment.

After looking at the options, no matter how emotional I feel, we will not be booking a ticket back to our home country. Knowing this is very risky because not being able to get home is now my reality since the flight just sold out. However, the cons of traveling home on the next flight outweigh the risks of staying. We will continue to self-isolate on the quiet hill in the Costa Rica jungle as we monitor the crisis.

To my parents and kids, please remember no matter what happens, it's not the end of the world. I will never joke about it again. The world just has bigger problems than me right now, so I will not be coming home at this time. Missing each and every one of you. I promise to return home as soon as it's safe for me to travel.

Most of the World is Sleeping
April 10, 2020

Writing in the dark jungle while the rest of the world sleeps is my favorite time of day.

Now I don't know about you, but I was never a morning person. One thing is for sure, that changed shortly after we relocated to Costa Rica. Now, I could tell you it's because the jungle is loud in the mornings, or the country goes to bed at an early hour. I'm not kidding you, sunset at the beach is around 5:30 and many are in bed shortly after the sun hits the water.

When we first moved, most mornings Steve and I would wake up and have our morning coffee while sitting out on our porch. Often, we would take a stroll on the beach as we watched the world come to life. Beach walking in the morning is the best very little people also a great time to see interesting wildlife. We have seen everything from turtles being born, sea snakes, sea urchins, and even a baby octopus these are just a few of the amazing creatures.

Most of these mornings would start around 5:00 am with Steve encouraging me to get up and move my body before it was too hot outside. To say I was a fan of waking up at this time would be a complete lie. I still hated get-

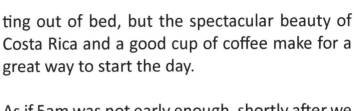

ting out of bed, but the spectacular beauty of Costa Rica and a good cup of coffee make for a great way to start the day.

As if 5am was not early enough, shortly after we started writing our first book the coffee started coming around the 3am hour. This time of morning has always been a weird time of day for me. It's usually the time I wake up and can't go back to sleep. You know those nights when you wake up and toss and turn for hours trying to fall back to into a dream world.

This is when my brain seems to want to work in overdrive. I obsess over things that most of the time, I have no control over. If I was lucky, I would usually get back to sleep right before the alarm clock would go off, making waking up that much harder. So instead, I welcomed a hot cup of coffee and writing seemed to be something that I enjoyed.

It did not take long not even a month into the writing process when I found myself springing out of bed at this crazy hour ready to start the day. Instead of tossing and turning with my thoughts this hour was now full of writing, and research. I learned everything I could on how I was going to publish once we finished the manuscript.

The world is beautiful while it sleeps. It's so quiet, I can hear the ocean break on the rocks. This sound is usually drowned out by the sounds of people or even the wildlife. Like I said the jungle is loud. The roar of the loudest

land animal, the howler monkeys, will ring out in about 20 minutes waking up the rest of the world.

My world has been on lock-down for 23 days. Today will be another day of no people. While trying to stay focused, I find myself thankful for feeling like getting up and writing. I have been doing this every morning for years now. Early mornings are part of my daily routine; it happens without an alarm clock. This special time of day is priceless but let's face it, with lock-down motivation is starting to fall to the wayside. I can't wait until the world opens again.

Everyone is Starting to Move Back!!!
April 11, 2020

Most of my friends are going home, even the ones that have been here for decades!

I woke up to this from a friend today.

"There's a rumor going around that your next book is "Cut the Crap Costa Rican's and move back to Colorado" but you know how rumors are."

Currently, we have no intention of going home, but it is a hot topic. Man, it sucks watching my expat friends go back to their home counties. I watch them struggle to get flights and liquidate assets from homes to cars and even a business. My heart breaks that over a handful of my friends many who have been here for decades, will all fly out on the next repatriation flight.

One of the things I must ask myself is what are we going to do? The majority of our support system has left the country. Most of those that remain are talking of going home or to other countries. If something were to happen to us, I don't know who I would call. When living abroad a good support system is essential.

It is hard to watch our support system fly away.

Our Remote Paradise
April 13, 2020

Stores & businesses are being affected. The government has mandated the closure of borders, beaches, parks, schools, bars, churches, and strict driving restrictions have been implemented. Restaurants are allowed to open with strict guidelines, some are offering take-out orders while most have just closed.

Currently, I have been self-isolating with my husband and daughter with no contact with the outside world for 26 days. This has provided some peace of mind when trying to stay healthy during these uncertain times. However, we still need to eat and that requires a trip to town. This is needed more than ever since both the bread and fruit trucks have not delivered in over 2 weeks. It is about the same drive time to both Santa Cruz in the south or Villar-eal to the North.

It has been a couple of weeks since my last supply run, and the food is starting to run low. No matter how much I don't want to go to town, it's necessary. Whether I want to or not, today I'm going to find out how all of this is affecting the stores and businesses.

Jumping into the passenger seat of Buffy's Isuzu truck, I prepare for the shopping. She's a Cali

Expat and has been living here with her husband for the last couple of years. Her husband is what I would call a seasoned expat, having lived here for decades. Over the last year, she has become my ride-or-die buddy when it comes to shopping.

She exhales a deep breath as she asks, "Are you ready for this?"

My response is a quick "NO, are you?"

Both of us roll our eyes and chuckle as we do our show and tell of what we are bringing on our adventure. I brought a bottle of hand sanitizer and she brought disinfectant wipes. These items are something that both of us had on hand before all the crazy started. I always travel with a little bottle of sanitizer clipped to my bag especially when traveling internationally.

Neither of us has been to town for a couple of weeks so we have no clue what the bigger stores were going to be like. I have been in contact with some friends in Tamarindo the past couple of days who have informed me the streets are empty. They reported that the store's shelves have food, personal hygiene products including soaps, cleaning supplies, and toilet paper.

We choose to head towards Villareal because that is where our favorite fruit stand and veterinarians are, and as I said, the reports from Tama were good, so why not.

We Need to Stock up a bit

Most of the time our goal is to stock up for a week or two. Since it takes about an hour one way, both of us try to limit the trips. This time the goal is much different. This time our goal is to have as little contact with others while stocking up for a whole month if possible. Risking exposure is scary in itself, but having an autoimmune condition makes this trip even scarier.

How quickly can we get in and out of the stores? As much as we want to get it all done in one stop, it's just not possible with the way we shop here. We have been doing this trip every week for almost a year now, so we know exactly where we have to go. It's going to take at least five stops to get everything. This brings my anxiety level even higher than normal, but it needs to be done no matter how much it worries me.

I do want to note Steve did offer to go instead of me. I decided to go myself because even if he got sick, he would most likely give it to me since we are in the same bubble. Hands down this girl can shop quicker than him since this is my department, limiting exposure to our household.

1st Stop ComeFruta Feria in Villareal

As we pull into our first stop at the ComeFruta feria in Villareal, the signs are all over the front of the building.

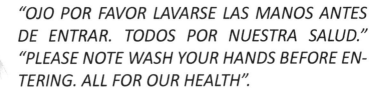

"OJO POR FAVOR LAVARSE LAS MANOS ANTES DE ENTRAR. TODOS POR NUESTRA SALUD." "PLEASE NOTE WASH YOUR HANDS BEFORE ENTERING. ALL FOR OUR HEALTH".

A hand-washing station with sink, soap, and running water have been installed outside of the feria. This is a big surprise since running water and sinks are not something you see on the outside of a building let alone an outside fruit market in a developing country. It is a huge step in the right direction of giving me a little peace of mind.

Watching people line up to wash their hands before heading into the market, I feel a little better about what the day is going to hold. After both of us wash our hands, we head in to grab our supplies. The stands are full of fresh fruits and vegetables with no shortages in sight. It takes less than five minutes for both of us to fill our carts and checkout.

Note: No one, including us, is masked in this store.

2nd Stop Maxi Pali

The next stop is Maxi Pali. This is like a Mini-Walmart where we can buy our non-perishable items and personal hygiene products. They also carry produce and have a bakery, but just like in the states I like buying these products from the locals and smaller shops. As we walk through the door, once again we are greeted with signs,

spray bottles, and a roll of paper towels.

"Uso EXCLUSIVO para disinfection de coches y canastas. NO utilizar en el cuerpo." "EXCLUSIVE use for disinfection of carts and baskets. DO NOT use on the body."

We spray and wipe down the carts. After we are done, both of us use my hand sanitizer since what they provided was only for the carts, then off to shop. The store shelves are full but some items like cereal, cleaning supplies, and TP are limited to three per customer/household.

We approached the checkout aisle; the store had installed plexiglass separating the customer from the cashier. You are still expected to bag your groceries. After I pay the cashier, I step over and start bagging my groceries. Once he completes printing my receipt, the cashier joins in to help bag the remaining items. Reaching for one of my cloth bags, his hand accidentally bumps my arm...

Cause for Alarm

On a normal day, there would have been no cause for alarm; however, with the threat, this day is different. Immediately hitting an alarm, he takes two steps back and puts his hands in the air as if he was in a stick-up and I was the perpetrator. Once again, I speak very little Spanish and cannot understand any of the words that he is announcing extremely fast.

Let's call it what it is, Nikki is about ready to have a panic attack as his words get louder and louder.

"Come on girl get your crap together!"

Another employee comes running over to immediately relieve him of his duties at the cash register. Rushing directly to the bathroom, he leaves the door open. We stand watching him wash his hands with soap and water. I feel like the kiss of death. There's nothing like making a whole store standstill as they watch my scene play out. Even though he had just touched all the products that I had just touched and would not have washed after. I guess, it is a relief knowing that they are using proper hygiene after physical touch. It also gave us something to laugh about all day.

Note: A couple of older people were wearing masks. I even got a laugh at the old man wearing rubber gloves and mask who got in his truck and touched everything with the gloves that he has just gone shopping with.

Tip: Don't forget your reusable bags. This store charges for plastic bags that are so cheap you can't even line your bathroom trash can with them.

3rd Stop Mega Super

We throw non-perishables in the truck and proceed to use hand sanitizer before heading to our next stop, Mega Super. There's no ATM in the Marbella area, meaning if you need to get cash out of the ATM to pay the water and electric bill (that will only accept cash), it requires a trip to town. Walking into the store, we are greeted by a gentleman holding a spray bottle while standing next to a table with paper towels.

The store requires that he spray our cart and our hands before we can enter. The ATM is inside at the front of the store. I'm grateful that there is cash in the machine because these machines are notorious for running out of cash around the first and middle of the month when everyone gets paid. Exiting the store, the gentleman offers to spray my hands down again and I continue to wait outside while Buffy grabs a few supplies from inside. When she comes out, she informs me that the store shelves are also fully stocked just like they always have been.

No one was wearing a mask.

4th Stop DR. Cavallini Vets Office

The next stop is the veterinarian to pick up Heartworm and flea and tick medicine for our furry friends. Approaching Dr. Cavallini's office, there is a sign with a roll of paper towels sitting on a table with a spray bottle out-

side the front door, which is also locked. The employee is required to come around the front desk where she proceeds to unlock the door. Cracking it open, she asks me what I need.

Only after I spray my hands will she allow me to enter the building, locking the door right behind me. Making sure to keep a good distance from me while ringing up my items, she unlocks the door allowing me to leave. I see her squirt hand sanitizer for herself before sitting down.

Just like me no mask.

5th Stop Centro De Carnes Villa Mar in Villa Real

Meat is something that we have cut out of our diet almost completely since we wrote our cookbook; however, it is something that we like to have around when we do a BBQ. Not knowing when the next trip will be, we have a quick conversation about needing meat.

Both of us like to buy our meat and dog bones at the local carnicerìa. The carnicerìa was not on our list of stores to go to since we are trying to limit our exposure; however, neither of us have meat at home. We both feel business owners are doing a good job of making sure things are sanitary.

Tip: The Carnicerìa stocks Mike's Hot Sauce from the Jalapenos in Playa Negra. Hands down he makes some of the best hot sauce in the world. I highly recommend the "Que

Mango" and "Da Kind" flavors.

Just like the other stores, there is a table with a sign, spray bottle, paper towels, and they even have a bottle of hand sanitizer. A big sign is on the front door stating only four people are allowed in at a time. All the employees not only have their mouths covered but also their faces and heads fully covered. All you can see is their eyes. Everyone, including the lady at the register, has on latex gloves.

The store was at capacity and only employees were masked. I am thinking about how covered the employees were. Many reports are saying that this came from someone eating a bat in China.

Now before I eat the meat I wonder if COVID is a zoonosis virus, it would make sense? Is my food going to make me sick? Heck are the dog bones even safe?

6th Stop Groupo Economico

With meat and bones packed in the cooler, we venture on over to our last big stop, Groupo Economico. Again, greeted with much of the same. This store: also referred to as the Chinese store due to its primarily Chinese staff and products, has put big white boxes between the cash registers and the customers to ensure proper distance.

This store consistently has the cheapest dog food and juice. However, this is not the case when the next bag is bought, and they are completely out of the juices.

All but one of the employees are wearing surgical masks and have on latex gloves. Squirting another blob of hand sanitizer, we head back to the truck and are ready to head home, or are we?

While the employees are masked none of the customers were. Note, all employees have been masked since February and most have even been masking since December. I suspect this is due to the outbreak in China since late last year and the Chinese are notorious for masking.

Extra Stop Mini Super Villa Real

Last but not least on our shopping tour was the Mini Super Villa Real. While this is not a must, I really want my glass bottle of Coke and both of us need something to eat for the car ride home. Walking up to the store, you can see the line of people standing out front. The store has plumbed a sink with running water to create a handwashing station out in front with a soap bottle, and paper towels. An employee stands at the door to make sure everyone washes their hands and keeps distance between each other.

Only four people were let in at a time and I felt out of place when he jumped us to the front of the line. This is

something that doesn't happen. Usually, it's the other way around with others cutting in line, not me. Grabbing the cold glass bottle of Coke, we have a quick discussion about whether to risk the local homemade empanadas in the warming case. If you've ever eaten one of these empanadas you can appreciate the temptation. It only took a second for both of us to decide the risk was worth it. I even risked the hot homemade peppers and onions!

Just like the other stores, they wanted us to stand back away from the cashier, so they have placed a crate on the floor in front of the registers.

No one has a mask.

Let's Head Home

With the truck loaded and road snacks bought, we do one last hand sanitizing and take off for home. Relaxing and enjoying the beautiful scenery, we feel great relief having completed our supply run. We both express our pride in our efficiency. Both of us share how impressed we are with the precautions that the various businesses are taking. It's a relief to see that the country is serious about protecting itself.

There were a few things that stood out to me from my day of shopping in Costa Rica during the pandemic. First, all the stores were fully stocked with their respective

items. There were not even shortages of disinfectants or TP. Second, every one of them was taking precautions.

The smaller stores seemed increasingly vigilant with even higher precautions as they had plumbed running water with sinks and soap not just spray bottles. In addition, most stores had employees ensuring everybody sanitized their hands while limiting the number of people in the stores at one time.

I'm happy that we chose to ride this out in paradise. Unlike many countries, Costa Rica is taking the situation seriously. Thank you to the stores and government for doing your part to keep people safe during this time of uncertainty.

Can I Legally Drive?
April 14, 2020

With driving restrictions in place and borders closed, I question whether I can legally drive in this country anymore!

My visa stamp in my U.S. passport expired on April 2, 2020. Due to the state of emergency, the Costa Rica government extended my visa to May 17, 2020, but I did not get a new stamp in my passport. Reaching out to the attorneys I ask if the extension includes driving privileges.

Currently, they are unable to answer my question. They informed me that they have contacted the government for clarification so at the moment they do not have an answer. Nobody can answer my question, but the general response is to drive at your own risk.

There is a difference between Immigration and the Ministry of Public Works and Transport (MOPT) who controls driving laws. Just because immigration has changed its rule regarding length of stay doesn't mean that MOPT has changed its rules regarding how long your out of country license is valid. Traditionally it has been linked to the number of days written on your tourist visa.

Does anyone want to take bets? This chica puts all her money on NO, I don't think I can! Most people in chat groups are disagreeing with me. Would you risk it?

What are the Risks

The number of checkpoints has increased drastically throughout the country over the last few weeks. There is a high likelihood I will be stopped at a checkpoint, at which point they would check my plate number and ensure I have current RITEVE and Marchamo stickers.

RITEVE is a vehicle inspection that is required each year for all street-legal vehicles including trucks, cars, motorcycles, scooters, four-wheelers, etc. This inspection primarily focuses on the safety features of the vehicle, such as lights, seatbelts, tires, horns, and general operation of the vehicle. To complete the inspection, you must make an appointment at the RTV office. You can call one of the offices to schedule the inspection, or you can schedule it online at the RTV official website by entering a telephone number and the vehicle's license plate number.

As in the United States, there are legal requirements on vehicles using the public roads in Costa Rica. Marchamo is similar to paying a yearly license plate tax in the U.S. It includes the taxes, registration, and basic liability insurance required for each vehicle. Payment of the Marchamo is due between November 1st to December 31st of each year. There are relatively high penalties for late payment and high fines if stopped by a transito and the Marchamo

is expired.

I would be asked to show my driver's license and a copy of my passport and last visa stamp. This is a typical stop and happens all the time. They could also ask to see my fire extinguisher and safety vest. After dozens of stops over the years, we have never been asked to show these last two items but it's the law to have them in your car. Over the years I have talked to many who have received tickets for not having them.

Note we have never had to show them to pass the RITEVE inspection either.

In our first book, "Cut The Crap & Move To Costa Rica", we talk about how you can use a photocopy of your passport and stamp. This was recommended by an officer when we arrived and has worked for years; however, the law has changed due to the world going to crap.

You now must show your passport where they will look at the stamp. If the officer does not like my expired stamp, even though it has been extended through immigration, they can remove my license plates or even impound the vehicle. Fines for these types of violations have been raised due to the state of emergency. Trying to get a car out of impound or your plates back is a whole different set of problems and costly.

I will not drive as I have not received clear legal advice. This is the safest thing for me to do right now. Steve on the other hand would gamble and drive, but his passport has a valid stamp, so it is a moot point.

How Quickly can you Move Countries?
April 15, 2020

If the country keeps the borders closed and does not extend my visa, I will be forced to travel to another country and denied access back until the travel ban has been lifted. Nicaragua is our closest open border and is not currently mass testing for COVID-19. The reports that I'm getting say people in Nicaragua are dying at alarming rates, but I'm being told it's not being reported on the news. The high health risk of traveling at this time concerns me. If the extension doesn't happen, I will be forced to leave the country due to an expired visa. Currently, I pray that the government extends my tourist visa, so I don't have to travel.

Yet another concern is the talk of the local hospitals filling up and the government making us leave because they cannot offer us care even if we are willing to pay out of pocket for it. It is understandable as Costa Rica is a small country, and the hospitals can only care for a certain number of patients.

I'm scared because flight prices have almost tripled for a flight back to the U.S. The extended visas for my daughter and I will expire on "May 17, 2020". This leaves us with only 32 days left on the extended visas. Steve's visa stamp expires on June 15, 2020. The government is hoping to re-open the borders for travel on April 30, 2020. However,

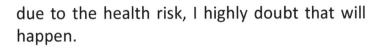

due to the health risk, I highly doubt that will happen.

I will never look at the world the same again as I continue to self-isolate with my husband and daughter. At this time, we are all healthy and happy here, so we try to find the little joys throughout day-to-day life while looking forward to new travels and adventures when things have settled down.

Chica, 32 days is just not enough time to move to a different country. Every day you wait is going to make it harder, and I don't think this is going to be over any time soon.

Holiday Restriction
April 16, 2020

Last week was Semana Santa, also known as Holy Week. The holiday starts the weekend before Easter and continues through Easter Sunday. In previous years, during this time, the locals from the big city of San Jose take their holiday breaks and flock to the sandy beaches where they enjoy partying and surfing. The restaurants and bars are packed as families spend time together while they enjoy their meals and drinks.

This reminds me of Florida over spring break where the beaches become overrun with college kids on holiday except it doesn't include just young college kids. Families of all ages from the young to the old come out to partake in these festivals.

Not This Year

This year, closures and restrictions have caused the cancellation of all holiday events.

The government not only halted alcohol sales which is common in certain cantons during this time of year, but they also forced the stop of liquor sales in nearly all cantons across the country. The closure of all beaches and borders has been extended. Public and private transportation vehicles were told when and where they were

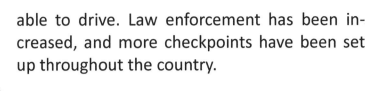

able to drive. Law enforcement has been increased, and more checkpoints have been set up throughout the country.

The beaches remain empty and guarded by law enforcement. I'm not kidding you; police officers have shot their weapons to get surfers out of the water! *(Thomas)* The incident went viral and last I heard the officer was fired. In addition, fines for breaking any of these laws have been increased, some of them more than double the previous amount. Some people have reported being ticketed hundreds of dollars.

The government did an amazing job of slowing down tourism over the holiday weekend. The majority of people chose to stay in the city, however, some decided to jump in their car heading out on their vacation destinations before the restrictions were implemented. For the most part, the beach towns looked like a ghost town, not spring break.

New driving restrictions state that vehicles will be allowed on the roads only for going to the supermarket, pharmacy, or health centers, and again limited by license plate numbers. I'm not allowed to drive my personal automobile from 7 pm to 5 am. Since my plate number ends in a 3, I'm not allowed to drive on Tuesdays and Sundays.

There are more infected people in the city, so this caused me to put off this week's supply run because of the higher risk. We have enough beans and rice, and packaged foods

to make it until next week. Just like last week, we still did not have any food delivery trucks.

I want to note Steve's favorite food is beans and rice. This chica has learned there are a million different dishes this can be used in. I have never been so thankful to have beans and rice.

Here's what's for dinner tonight. Get your free recipe from our International Best-Selling Cookbook.
https://theultimatecostarica.com/recipes/tostada-with-refried-beans

Bootleggers
April 17, 2020

It has been 28 days since the stop of alcohol in our canton.

Wow, it's starting to sound like the stories of the 1930s during the Great Depression. What I would do to have a night cap with Mommy Hay and talk about what's going on around the word.

Things I never thought I would see in my lifetime, let alone consider partaking in. But let's face it Steve and me would both like a drink and the house has been dry for weeks. Once again, I tried to tell him that one small bottle was not going to be enough when they stopped alcohol sales. I believe the words I used were "we should stock up on liquor".

In his defense we try not to drink a lot and having bottles around the house while being in lock-down might prove to be too tempting. While my friends in Colorado are reporting they can now pick mixed drinks up as a take-out order from the local restaurants. The country that allowed me to buy a drink in a to-go-mug now is dry except for a couple of cantinas high in the jungles.

What does it take to get to the Tilaran area? This trip

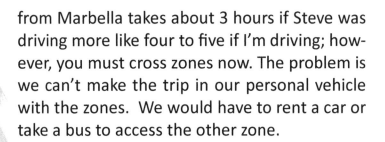

from Marbella takes about 3 hours if Steve was driving more like four to five if I'm driving; however, you must cross zones now. The problem is we can't make the trip in our personal vehicle with the zones. We would have to rent a car or take a bus to access the other zone.

This issue makes this trip expensive and time consuming. For me it's not worth it for a bottle of liquor. People in group chats are offering to bootleg it in and sell it at a little higher cost. Some refer to it as a handling fee or donation, lol. I ask myself if we want to order some liquor before, they leave in the morning.

What I would do for a mixed drink next to the pool. After a long talk with Steve our house will stay dry. We will see what happens next time they do a run.

I Need Help!!!
April 18, 2020

My husband just told me he's "NOT" my secretary. Solution, we need to hire more help.

It's never easy!

I hate editing, third round and the manuscript is still bleeding!

As an added stress, I'm mad at my husband who seems to not be showing up for anything, not wanting to write or even help with the editing. My close girlfriends that I have shared this with keep asking me if he is going through a mid-life crisis. My response back has been NO WAY but let's face it, he is in his mid 40's and our last child is about to graduate. Plus, she has been talking about moving back to the states for months. I am sure this is weighing on him just as much as it has been weighing on me.

We have been married for over 20 years, but not without children since both of us brought a child into the marriage and our son Ellis was born shortly after we had wed.

From one chica to another, all I can say is if he is going to have a breakdown, this would be the time. If he is ready to walk away from writing or even this life, now is the time

to get it out. No matter how much we don't like it, we are going to be empty nesters soon. Life has many possibilities. I hope he wants me to come along on whatever journey he takes; but in reality, I need to be honest with myself. My dreams are big and include a lot of international travel.

Over the years he has been saying that he doesn't want to travel, he has found his paradise. While I'm happy for him, there is still a lot of the world I want to see, and I have been banking on him coming along. Now that he is giving me a hard time about publishing, maybe it's time I jump off this ship. I'm not talking about a marriage divorce, more like a business divorce. Familiar territory we've done this a couple of times over the decades with the multiple business we have owned.

Remember, you are the author of your story. It's ok to change the ending right up to the final deadline. How do you want to see the story end? One of the things I learned when we did our move was its ok to mourn the way you thought the book was going to be written. I learned this from watching how hard it was for my husband to let go of things like cars, tools, and even our home. Everything that the man had worked all his life for had to be sold.

It was painful to watch; however, what happened next was beautiful. From healing our relationship to becoming better parents, the eye-opening life of living in Costa Rica has forever changed us on so many levels.

One thing is for sure, I know that no matter what we'll make it through as we both grow and change. It just might take a little bit of time to figure it all out.

He Moved Out
April 19, 2020

My days are bleeding together. No matter how much I thought this was not going to affect us, it is. One thing I know to be true, Steve is my partner in crime, but we are not meant to be together 24 hours a day.

Over three and a half decades of knowing this amazing man, this chica can call myself an expert on this relationship. Especially considering two of those decades being his wife and work partner in multiple businesses adventures, all while raising four children.

When all of this started, jokes about being a divorce attorney and how much they were going to make off the pandemic were common. We need some distance; however, I did not think that he would pack his stuff and move into the other cabina. I guess the work divorce has started.

The one thing I can say is, he has been so negative about everything that he needs a time out anyway. Let's be honest, he has been affecting the mojo in the main house with all his negativity. Remember there are always two sides to the story. I'm sure his side will tell you I need the time out. Maybe he is right either way we need to go to our own corners for a while.

I will give him his space. He will return when he is ready.

We Have to Eat
April 20, 2020

We have to eat and no one, not even the local transit-os have been able to answer my question over the last week.

My fresh fruits and vegetables are running low, and these are major staples of our diet. We have been eating a lot more processed foods like hot dogs, pasta, and potato chips. These foods are not what we normally eat, but it has allowed us to not have to go to the store as much since these foods last longer than fresh food. The bread truck that comes to our casa every Monday has not delivered in over 4 weeks while the produces at the mini supers looks awful. In all fairness, the fruit trucks have also disappeared.

All of this is having a negative effect on our health. Since the lock-down has begun, I've gained 5 pounds, my MS has also been acting up more causing both digestive problems and more muscle pain than the norm. I find happiness in the fact that I have a couple of bags of pasta, beans, and rice.

I do what I call a "happy dance" when I check the coffee and dry creamer to discover I have enough to last for 7 days. This allows me to enjoy a cup during my writing

time or morning calls to my family back in the states. The little stores in town do not have our favorite coffee and most of the time only have the creamer that tastes like cardboard.

It's been 18 days since my stamp expired and the government still has not got back to the attorneys or the embassy regarding driving privileges. I don't mind walking to the store but it's about ¾ of a mile to the market and carrying back groceries is not something I like to do.

Question Answered

Expats Can't Drive!

We just received our attorney's response. I CAN NOT drive due to an expired visa stamp. Even though the visa date for stay has been extended the driving privileges have not. Never assume that one thing is linked to another. Immigrations and driving (MOPT) are two different departments.

This is just part of the Pura Vida Life!

COVID-19 Status
April 21, 2020

When we look at the stats, Costa Rica seems to be taking a positive turn. For so many weeks we heard discouraging reports of incredible growth and spread of the virus globally. Those reports have been echoed here as well.

Recent days and weeks have started telling a different story. Not one of despair but rather a story of hope and positive change. The status seems to be turning a corner.

18 Days With no new Cases in Guanacaste

The last reported case in the Guanacaste province came from the canton of Hojancha on April 3, 2020. Hojancha is located in the center of the Nicoya Peninsula of Costa Rica. Since then, no new cases have been received by the Ministry of Health from the 12 cantons of Guanacaste. That is over 18 days ago.

Guanacaste is known for its tourism. It holds what is known as the Gold Coast, a strip of popular beaches with stunning beauty. The lack of new cases is good news for the tourism industry and the large expat community of Guanacaste.

11 of 13 Already Recovered

There is almost 100% recovery! The Guanacaste prov-

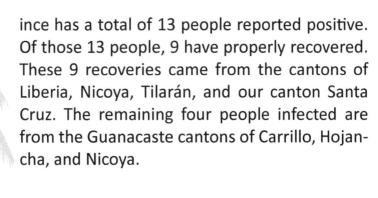

ince has a total of 13 people reported positive. Of those 13 people, 9 have properly recovered. These 9 recoveries came from the cantons of Liberia, Nicoya, Tilarán, and our canton Santa Cruz. The remaining four people infected are from the Guanacaste cantons of Carrillo, Hojancha, and Nicoya.

Total Costa Rica Cases

Costa Rican health authorities have reported a total of 669 cases. With a total population of approximately 5 million people that is an extremely small percentage of the population (.01%). Cases have been reported in 59 cantons of the seven provinces of Costa Rica.

Infected, Recovered, and Lost

Here's the breakdown of the 669 infected people. Of the 669 infected, **150 have already recovered.** The Alajuela canton boasts the most recovered patients with 36 currently ill, while only **11 are hospitalized** and 6 are in intensive care. The intensive care patients range in age from 44-75.

Regrettably, 6 people have been lost due to the virus. All six fatalities were males ages 45-87 years old. There were two 87-years-old, a 45-year-old, an 84-year-old, and most recently 69 and 54 years old.

Testing

There have been 11,387 People Tested. Fortunately, 7,495 of the tests came bacP negative. The country continues to test individuals showing symptoms. A personal friend had an asthma exacerbation that displayed common symptoms. They were tested within 24 hours at no charge in their home by representatives of the Ministry of Health to be sure they were not infected.

Precautions and Closures are Still in Place

Earlier this week, the Minister of Health, Daniel Salas, reported that the border closures to foreigners will remain in force until May 15th. Costa Rica is taking its response to this crisis seriously.

Our morning walks on the beach and days exploring national parks are on hold. The beaches and public areas remain closed. There is a stay-at-home order in place.

Driving restrictions continue, limiting days people can travel based on license plate numbers, and no one can drive at night. No more joyriding and spying on the beautiful landscape of Costa Rica. Even when Steve can drive, we are limited as to where we can go.

Every effort is being made to slow and hopefully stop the spread. This country cannot afford to under-react. The majority of people are following the directives and the

police are actively enforcing them.

The status looks promising. The growth curve is flattening out and seems to be stabilizing. The number hospitalized is down two people from yesterday. Every day reports of recoveries are shared. We are not through this crisis yet but there are reasons for hope.

No Work
April 23, 2020

"Mom, both of us have been laid off!" These were the words during our morning coffee with our daughter Morgan. She and her boyfriend had been working at a llama farm where they had been considered essential workers.

"We are not for sure our boss is gone to qualify for the funding, but he told us he was going to try to get us furloughed when he let us go. He was as brutal as he could be when saying we might not get paid next month, what should I do?" These were the words that I could make out between the crying.

In the last few days, both her sister and brother's calls had resembled much of the same. Having no job to report to were now circumstances that all our adult children had to face.

She informed me she had been waiting on hold for over five hours to get her paperwork done for unemployment and just like yesterday the line would eventually cut out.

"Keep trying" were my words as she continued with her breakdown, saying that this was now her third day sitting on hold and her boss was giving up on his side of the paperwork.

"Mom I can't pay my bills next month what should I do?"

"All I can do is tell you to start looking at online jobs or front-line work while you sit on hold. Think outside of the box and find the businesses that are doing something to adapt. They will be the ones to keep their doors open!"

What are You Doing for Dessert?
April 25, 2002

Here's what I'm making.
Instead of reaching for candy and baked goods, why not grab a serving of plantains? They are nutritious and can curb your sweet tooth.

One of Steve and Taya's favorite treats, fried plantains they are a scrumptious and very affordable treat. They can be eaten as snacks, sides, and even desserts. A staple to the Costa Rican diet; this delicious fruit can be found on most casados (typical Costa Rican plates). Fried Plantains make a great side and add color and sweetness to an otherwise bland plate.

Get my favorite fried plantain Recipe here:
https://theultimatecostarica.com/recipes/fried-plantain

Needs vs Wants
April 26, 2020

It is almost May, and our lease will be up soon. The owners have mentioned they may be coming to stay here to get away from the pandemic in the United States. I have to find a place for us to stay in case they are able to fly in soon. Unlike in the states, it is somewhat difficult to search for rentals. Especially those special deals that few people know about. One of the ways we have been able to maintain our budget here is because we found great deals on housing.

As I begin my search, I have to really research each property. Sometimes what looks like a jewel turns out to be a lemon come rainy season and the place is flooded. Or infestations that are not visible in the pictures they put online. One of the biggest issues we have had in Costa Rican homes is water.

Need and want are two very different words! With that said, I don't need hot water in my sinks. I do need hot water in my showers. Never thought this would be in the top 3 requirements when looking at homes, but as our lease is coming to an end on our vacation rental it's time to start looking at the next home. It's time to ask ourselves what we want because this will affect our budget; and let's be honest, with the world still locked down every penny counts. But this chica needs her hot water!

Hot Water and Showers in Costa Rica

Don't take hot water for granted! So, what is the water situation in Costa Rica?

It sounds pretty basic, considering the majority of North America has hot water in every faucet or at least every home. But that is not always the case here. There is a large percentage of homes that do not have hot water. In many homes that do, it's limited to only the shower or certain faucets.

We have visited and stayed in some homes that would be considered relatively upscale in the couple million-dollar range that did not have hot water. We jumped in the shower ready to relax but instead felt the invigorating flow of cold water covering our bodies.

It's not Like in the States

Every home we lived in back in the U.S. had a large water heater that provided hot water to the entire home. Having been real estate agents, we were all too aware of the need to ensure the tank is in good repair. On a handful of occasions, we even dealt with the issue of a leaking tank and even replaced a few.

A few friends back in the States have converted to the new technology of instant hot water heaters. However, they are not common at this time. I am jealous of these

friends and look forward to the day we can enjoy the benefits of these new advances in hot water technology.

Different hot Water Sources in Costa Rica

We have only seen a couple of the standard water heaters with the tank; however, most tanks are smaller. Our second condo had a small one that was about half the size of our home in the U.S. This unit was sufficient for our usage. The downside was that it heated the utility room and in turn the rest of the condo. Keeping the tank warm costs more in utilities than the more common instant hot water units.

Instant hot Water Units

Many of the homes we have lived in here had wall-mounted instant hot water units similar to the ones our friends in the States upgraded to. These units are capable of heating the water very quickly and to a very high temperature. You can adjust the max temperature of the water for comfort and safety. They use less electricity than the tank units and we definitely prefer them.

The last form of heating water that we have experienced we like to refer to as the "suicide shower". Using electricity directed through a coil, the water is heated just before delivery. We have seen a few of these units that looked perfectly safe to use. However, on some occa-

sions, the places we have visited have had heaters that were old and looked as though you would be showered with a lightning stream. This form of water heating is cheap to install so it is commonly found in lower-income housing or remote areas.

Tip: We are not sure if it is just miscommunication or poor workmanship, but we have experienced many instances where the hot and cold water are switched on the faucet. If you don't get hot water turn it the other way.

Our advice: if you feel you need hot water, be sure to ask if it is available. If you are not sure if it is a priority for you, try taking a few cold showers or washing your dishes with cold water and see if you feel you can do without it.

NO WATER

Now that we have hot water out of the way, let's talk about water. When you hear the words drought, not enough water, watering restrictions what do you think of? Before our move, I would tell you about the Colorado drought in early 2000.

We could only water our yards twice a week during the nights. The state was encouraging all of us to use as little water as possible. Teaching our young kids how to turn off the water when brushing their teeth and limiting shower times was a big deal in our house, but it never even crossed my mind what I would do if they just shut the water off.

Talk about culture shock, no water, ya, you heard me no water! I wish I could say I was joking, but this is no laughing matter. Especially in the dry season, it's normal for the water company to ration water. This means turning off the water to not only the small villages but also the bigger towns and even parts of the city.

To get around not having water, most places have water tanks. This is great, however, when you are in a condo or even some subdivisions and are fed water from one tank, this puts you at the mercy of others. The water problems were not as bad in Marbella as in Tamarindo, Langosta, and surrounding areas, but there are still problems.

Can you Drink the Water in Costa Rica?

I will never forget the first time my parents visited. We were sitting at an upscale restaurant when the waitress placed a cup of water in front of my dad and as he picked up the glass, his wife Deb pulled it out of his hands, yelling "What! Are you crazy? You can't drink that water!" Laughing at her while she wiped the water that she spilled all over her off, I mentioned that we were not in Mexico and the water was safe to drink and was not going to kill him.

Caution Drink the Water at Your Own Risk.

Pick your poison. We talk a lot about drinking water in our videos and blogs especially when traveling. Steve and I are both big water drinkers, but over the years we have tried to stay away from plastics as much as we can. Not only because of environmental reasons, but for health reasons since cancer has been linked to plastic, we try to avoid using the big 5-gallon plastic bottles that we have set up at our home as much as we can.

Costa Rica water is known for high levels of calcium. Let me tell you the calcium is a bitch to clean! Not only does it leave water spots on everything it is impossible to get off the bathroom fixtures and even my wedding rings ended up with calcium build-up. However, that was nothing compared to the kidney stones that Steve ended up with due to the high levers of calcium from the water he had been drinking.

It happened 3 weeks before we launched the cookbook "Cut The Crap Kitchen". I have never seen my husband so sick in my life. Excruciating pain, fever that lasted for over two weeks sent us running to the local clinic where he received x-rays, blood work, 2 bags of fluids multiple shots of pain meds, two antibiotic shots, and 12 days of oral antibiotics.

One of the upsides is the medical care at Beachside Clinic is amazing and the doctors and nurses were on top of

it. Waiting only 10 minutes to get an IV right after vitals, x-rays, and meds were done immediately. I know the bill would have cost us thousands in the U.S. however, the whole bill was less than $375.

So once again, remember to drink your water but pick your poison. To this day Steve still drinks Costa Rica water from the tap, but we do run it through a filter first.

At this moment we have not experienced any more water problems than normal. Just another reason I pray we don't have to move for a while. However, we could save about $500 a month in the house down the street. It is oceanfront property but doesn't have hot water. I'm sure Steve is willing to take cold showers and I would love to be right on the ocean. To me, I will pay the extra and give up the view for hot water.

Coming Out of Lock-down
April 28, 2020

Do you feel safe coming out of lock-down? This was the question I asked on my social pages today. As countries around the world start to lift bands and lock-down orders. Today I find myself asking, "Do I feel it's safe coming out of isolation?"

The doctors at Beach Side Clinic in Costa Rica yesterday announced, "April 27th COVID-19 Update: Costa Rica has 2 new confirmed cases since yesterday. There are currently no active cases in our area."

The closures were in hopes to slow down the spread. Looking at the numbers, it seems to be working.

Coming out

Yesterday the Costa Rica government announced that they were allowing certain things to open. Beaches are still closed; but public swimming pools, movie theaters, and non-contact sports will be allowed to start up again with strict rules. New guidelines will include the number of participants and times of operation.

So why am I not coming out of isolation yet?

History is why! Looking at what happened in 1918 with the Spanish flu and the number of sick worldwide, after things opened up the numbers spiked. The WHO and CDC are reporting on their website, 1-14 days incubation. One of my Costa Rica doctors said, "It could be even up to 22 days or more!" History is why COVID-19 has been compared to other pandemics like the Spanish Flu. If you look at history, there has always been a second wave.

I have spent the last 42-days self-isolating with my husband and daughter. We did this to make sure that we do not get sick and if we were infected, we would not spread the disease. The numbers in the country are extremely low and this gives me hope. However, I'm not a math genius, but it has only been 16 days since Easter weekend.

All it takes is one person from the city that was infected to have come in contact with someone in this area. To me, the risk is still too high. I will continue to self-isolate for at least 5-7 more days maybe longer, depending on what the numbers do this week.

More News From the Attorney
April 29, 2020

Just received an email from the attorney that I can now drive until July 17, 2020.

Driving in Costa Rica is just different!

Costa Rica is only 19,700 square miles (51,100 sq. km). Its length is 288 mi (464 km) N − S, and its width is 170 mi (274 km) E -W.

This is similar to driving from Denver, CO to Santa Fe, NM or Detroit, MI to Pittsburgh, PA and Detroit, MI to Cleveland, OH.

Costa Rica's size can be deceptive though. Most destinations are separated by only 50-100 miles (80-160 km) but can often take two to four hours to drive between them due to poor, or windy roads. The country is vast with rolling mountains, open plains, and lush river valleys. The amazing landscape is protected and as a result, prevents the construction of superhighways that would make the trip very quick.

The shape of Costa Rica is curved with the Caribbean Coast on the inside. Stretching a mere 132 mi (212 km); however, the northern Caribbean is made up of a series of rivers, estuaries, and mangrove forests that - aside from being protected - consists of terrain that is not easily built into roads.

The outer Pacific Coast is much longer at 801 mi (1,290 km) of curvy inlets, bays, and two additional peninsulas. The Nicoya Peninsula in the north is the larger one with many expat communities. Near the southern border you'll find the Osa Peninsula, named one of the most biologically intense places on earth by National Geographic some of which are not navigable by car.

The experience of driving in these various regions can vary drastically. The city of San Jose offers the traffic and congestion of New York while the jungle regions require river crossings, extreme potholes, and steep inclines. But let's not forget the times we simply beach hop the dirt backroads with the windows down just for fun.

Road Conditions

Being a developing country, there are few major cities, with more small to medium towns. Most local governments cannot afford the expense of paving roads. Asphalt and concrete highways are connecting all major areas, but once you leave the highway, the conditions can become very unpredictable.

Now that I can drive I just have to make sure to stay in my zone. I only drive on days that I'm allowed while only going to the grocery stores pharmacies, and doctors.

MAY 2020

Published
May 5, 2020

Another thing checked off the bucket list! I was published in a magazine. This is something I have wanted for a long time. Using some spare time during lock-down to write, I was able to get the big checkmark on this one. There are only a couple more things left on the bucket list. Almost time to start a new one.

Many of you have asked what happen to the parakeet, Captain Crunch Wrap. Here's the link to the digital article that was published in The Howler Magazine:

https://howlermag.com/the-day-a-bird-named-captain-crunch-came-into-our-lives/

This was an extremely hard piece since this chica is a how-to writer, not a creative story writer. I am sure you have tried some new things since you've had more time at home. For me, a different style of writing was my challenge. Challenge complete!

No Surprise
May 7, 2020

Borders will remain closed until June 15, 2020. It's hard to believe that 24 days has now turned into 50 days and the borders will remain closed for another 39 days. I'm so homesick! It's been 276 days since I have been home, but I still believe we made the right decision to stay here.

Let's call it what it is, the chances of taking our summer trip home to see my parents and kids is not likely. It's sad to say, but this has given me a whole new outlook when it comes to international travel and being away from family. I never thought I could be as home sick as I was during the first year of your relocation. No matter how prepared I thought I was, this has brought home sick to a new level.

I find it interesting that among our expat friends, this seems to be bothering more of the women than the men. Visits home are the hot topic during our ladies' nights that are now done over the Internet instead of in person at a local restaurant or paint night. It will be interesting to see how many people move back to their home countries in the coming months.

Healing Waters
May 18, 2020

I touched the ocean today. I'm excited because today is the day beaches open. Beaches have been closed for 59 days, and now some are allowed to open back up.

It's about 6:30 in the morning as I slowly make my way to pour the first cup of coffee. 99% sure that both Steve and Taya are going to join me, but they better get a move on if they want to ride with me. The beach is only open until 8 am and it's even more empowering because I can legally drive our personal vehicle. Not looking at the clock yet, but I know it's after 6 am.

I'm not even done pouring my coffee when Steve pulls up in what we refer to as "the Beast" our big blue Jeep. After 20 years of marriage, one would think he knows I'm not going without my morning cup of jo. On the other hand, after 3 decades of knowing this man, I know for a fact if I don't hurry up, I'm going to get left behind, so I grab the top to the Contigo that was holding my steamy coffee so I could head to the Beast.

Not wanting to be left behind, Taya comes running out of her cabina making sure that we realize she wants to come but is not quite ready. You can tell she is ready to swim while soaking up some sun in her bikini. I feel a little

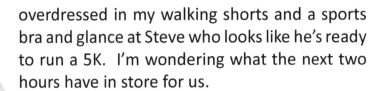

overdressed in my walking shorts and a sports bra and glance at Steve who looks like he's ready to run a 5K. I'm wondering what the next two hours have in store for us.

Costa Rica Barricades Ocean Entrances

The waves are getting louder as the Beast continues to drive down the bumpy dirt road. Overhead skies have a creepy feeling while the first morning light of the sun tries its hardest to shine through. Heavy grey clouds fill the thick humid air. It's not raining yet, but it just might before the day is over.

As we turn the corner, I can see the dirt barricade blocking the road. This particular barricade was put up right after the government closed the beaches. The big logs and tree trunks are piled up over the dirt. Rusty barbed wire holding it together was meant to keep people out. It reminds me of the old black and white war pictures my grandma would show us when I was a little kid.

CAN YOU SEE A WAY AROUND IT!

What I do know is I'm not breaking the law because Marbella is open from 5 am to 8 am Monday to Friday. Glancing down at the car clock I can see that it's a little before 7 am. Damn it, I'm living by a clock again and I only have 1 hour left.

Not knowing what's around the next corner, excitement from all of us could be felt. Even the dogs continue to

jump over Taya in the back seat. It's like a game of who could get the best window seats. Taya surrenders the window and takes the middle seat as each dog claims their window.

Our voices rang out at the same time "Can you see a way around it"? Taya was quick to remind us that she knows other ways down to the beach, but we would have to walk. Hearing the waves growing louder as we get closer, I'm going to walk if I have to. You can see where they have cleared just enough room for what looks like one car at a time to pull through. Looking up at Steve I can see that he's going for it.

Marbella beach in Costa Rica is open

There it is! It's literally a breath of fresh air, I can see the waves as the water splashes on the beach shores of Marbella. Surfers are off in the distance. I feel like a child jumping out of the Beast the minute Steve puts it into park. Embracing the sand between my toes, I take a little more time to look around than normal. I'm not scared of getting sick, but I have been in self-isolation with my family for 62 days. That's a long time for little contact with the outside world.

The numbers havebeen low

There have even been some days with no new active cases in our area. This makes me feel safe to start coming out. I do want to make sure that I keep a safe distance and don't really want to be around people. I'm ok with not talking to another person during this beach visit.

Waves splash the cool ocean water on my legs as Steve and I walk up and down the sandy beach. We can see a couple of small groups of surfers in the distance and yells of happiness ring out as they hit the water. To the single lady headed in the other direction, a simple wave and a hi from afar will do for today. On a different day, this encounter with a stranger might have been met with a conversation or maybe a new friendship would have been formed. But, not on this day as both parties respect their distance. Watching my child play on the beach with her dogs is priceless.

Not all Beaches Opened
Not all beaches opened today. The government started to slowly open the country as they continue to watch the numbers. Many beaches in national parks were not allowed to open today. There has also been some confusion as to whether people are allowed to swim and surf on beaches like Tamarindo, Playa Grande, and even Langosta because of the estuary. It will be interesting to see how the day plays out on these beaches. Are people going to try to surf and if so, how will the police handle it?

I Came out of Isolation in the Costa Rica Jungle to Touch the Ocean!

It has been 62 days since my family started self-isolation in the jungle to avoid getting sick. As Costa Rica slowly starts to come out of lock-down I'm slowly coming out of isolation. I have not been allowed to legally access the Costa Rica beach that is less than a quarter of a mile from my home for 59 days.

I realize my world has changed. I embrace the new world as I slowly start to come out of isolation.

Today, I touched an ocean!

JUNE 2020

Mind Changing
June 08, 2020

Today after 66 days of the fighting, the WHO & CDC are on the same page. *(Ellis)*

My friends who have not been masking were not going to put one on now without some push back. It's so sad to see what this is doing to friendships. The fighting that is going on worldwide is crazy, words like murderer and killer were being using even before these two organization said to mask.

While the people who are accused of the offenses are yelling "don't take my rights away," and " ony a 1% chance of fatality", the government is trying to control us and using the CDC as a puppet. The numbers are wrong.

I don't consider myself to be a conspiracy theorists, but to be really honest, the more I research trying to say they are wrong the more I start to see things their way. The world is really weird right now.

I have never been so lucky to live on a hill far away from people.

Riot and Protesting
June 10, 2020

Get out of the city!

The protesting and rioting erupted across the U.S. following the shooting of George Floyd, with the backing of "Black Lives Matter". The destruction of graffiti and burn piles left behind from the protesters leave a nasty taste in my mouth. Now this chica is always down for a good protest but burning buildings and business while destroying structures and monuments is disgusting in my opinion.

I'm no stranger to city living. As a matter of fact, I lived in what was referred to as 5 points in Denver and saw some crazy stuff go down, but this is anarchic shit that is happening. The news reports and pictures of Denver, Colorado are now added to the list of cities around the U.S. that have been shaken by the protesters. Listening to my friends and family talk about the annihilation of this beautiful city I'm dismayed.

The news gets even worse, as calls from family are reporting that the protesters are now in our hometown of Fort Collins. I pray that they are not allowed to burn down the beautiful city we grew up in.

God, please protect our friends, families, and their businesses. As a small business owner this is tragic to watch as people's livelihoods are being burned to the ground. If seeing it on social media was not enough, it has taken over all Costa Rica Spanish channels, now airing the U.S. news 24 hours a day. I'm turning off all the social media and tv, time for a good book.

Note, there has been a lot of protests in Costa Rica this is nothing new, but the violence is not the same as what is being reported from the U.S.

Stay in Your Zone
June 12, 2020

Over the months Costa Rica has gone into a tighter lock-down, mandating hotels, restaurants, beaches, you name it, close. Stopping both private and public transportation while dividing the country into zones that private and public vehicles are not allowed to cross has brought the country to a stop.

They also controlled what products people are allowed to buy in privately owned stores. During certain days of the week, private stores had to block off and stop sales of clothing, electronics, and other departments

My kids in the U.S. have reported having to go up and down aisles one way while shopping, but they are still able to shop for what they want and when they want it. This is in the big chain store. All the smaller, non-essential stores were forced to close. Most big stores that were open 24 hours a day are now closed during the night so they can clean and restock. Just like here the first couple of hours are reserved for the elderly.

The biggest thing that stands out to me is an attorney told me at the beginning of this that it was against the law for Costa Rica to make their people stay in their homes, that it was a violation of their civil rights. However, it seems it's not against the law to lock them in zones and stop them from shopping while closing down everything. I'm thinking out of the box and wondering if this is the way to get people to stay home or is it just a way to control what they are doing?

No HUGS!!!!
June 17, 2020

I'm starting to feel the effects of not being around people. It has been over 100 days since I have spent time with my friends.

Today there is no joy that my neighbor must stop in at the dentist. It only took me a minute to accept her offer of a ride to town, not because the food was running low, but this chica has alternative motives.

I have a gift for my dentist friend. The signed copy of our #1 International Best Seller has been sitting on my desk since I arrived back. It might just be enough to get me through the door at the office so I can see my friend.

Not only is Silvia Duran the best dentist I have found over the years, but she has also become one of my closest Tica friends. This year has kept us from our yearly girls' trip and there has been NO concerts in the big city or partaking in horseback riding, the hot springs, no hikes to the most amazing blue Waterfall Rio Celeste after a long night of girl talk. God, what I would do for a girl's trip to Bijagua right now.

Since this is just not possible, I will take my chances that she will have time to see me.

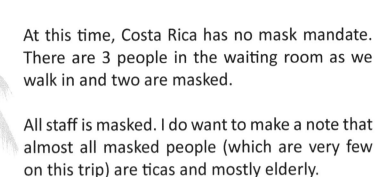

At this time, Costa Rica has no mask mandate. There are 3 people in the waiting room as we walk in and two are masked.

All staff is masked. I do want to make a note that almost all masked people (which are very few on this trip) are ticas and mostly elderly.

It was like a breath of fresh air as I heard her words "Nikki!"

Every inch of my body wanted to jump up and wrap my arms around my dearest friend who I had not seen in months.

She was doubled masked with not one but two surgical gowns on and what looked to be a layer under that. Both hands also looked to be double-gloved. Feeling my heart sink to the floor, the realization set in that she was risking her life just by showing up at work. Knowing she has a son who is high risk due to down syndrome makes this encounter even more uncomfortable.

I see the disappointment in her as both of us do an air hug. I'm sad that we could not take a picture of ourselves together with the book (thank you social distancing). I'm so thankful for the ten minutes of conversation we had. Even though it was not enough it would have to do for the day.

Remember to always be thankful for the little things; life

is short and could be over tomorrow. I tell myself; ten minutes is more than you had when you woke up.

Not only did it work to get me into the office, but she was also so pleased with the book she shared her thoughts on her profile.

> "How cool when your name appears in an amazon best seller, thanks Steve Page and Nikki Williamson-Page, glad you are happy with my work!!! is a blessing to have persons like you in my life!"

Sylvia, you're the best!

Should I Publish This?
June 18, 2020

Readers I need help. When reading history books would you rather read it as a diary or as a story? This was the question asked today on my social media pages.

The book title that had been scribbled out on the sticky note reads "24 Days Trapped in Paradise" The goal was to write a book during the 24 days of lock-down. Excited was an understatement! Talk about a dream come true! Days and nights filled with writing on a short deadline. Stocked up on coffee, and ready to accomplish the task.

The paper is still clinging to the back of the closet door 92 days later, reminding me every day that I need to write. This is something I do every day however since lock-down I have doubled down. I'm really starting to think I might publish this diary. The more I talk to my readers it seems to be something they would be interested in reading.

One thing is for sure, at this moment a travel guide to anywhere in the world is worthless right now! I can't wait until the world opens up and people get back to traveling.

24 Days Trapped in Paradise, or is it? As we enter the 92nd day of lock-down I ask myself if it's ever going to end? From being locked in zones to being told what we

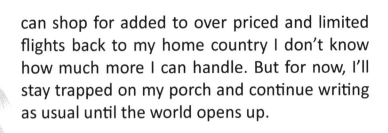

can shop for added to over priced and limited flights back to my home country I don't know how much more I can handle. But for now, I'll stay trapped on my porch and continue writing as usual until the world opens up.

Re-Opening Postponed!
June 19, 2020

#breakingNews

Churches and beaches will not be able to open this weekend. Return to driving restrictions that had been put into place over Holy Week (Easter) will take place again. The weekend's opening of theaters, museums, and shops is postponed.

20 years ago, I was an extrovert but now I'm a homebody and don't get out much except special events like Easter dinner with our church family. Not seeing the world for me has been hard and I can't imagine what this is doing to people who are type-A personalities.

It has been 93 days of no friends. To say canceling our small holiday gathering that was going to happen outside was sad would be an understatement. I really don't believe humans were made to stay away from each other how much more can the world handle. If this chica is missing people, others must be going crazy.

Mask Mandatory
June 22, 2020

Costa Rica announces masks are mandatory starting Saturday, June 27th. This has been the case for our family in the states for months.

Now I really don't want to go out. No face diapers for me! It is just another reason to stay away from the world, I guess.

It will have been 14 days from the day the WHO said to mask before Costa Rica mandated it.

None of this makes sense! Five days before we have to start masking. If masks help so much, why are they waiting? Is the government going to tell people the dangers about masks? Mask mouth, long term long lung problems, and even headaches are just some of my concerns.

I can't even imagine what this is going to do to our immune systems. The people around the world are cleaning and disinfecting everything around them.

Now they are even going to stop breathing the fresh air. How will their bodies develop immunities?

To top it all off the Costa Rica government thinks it's safer

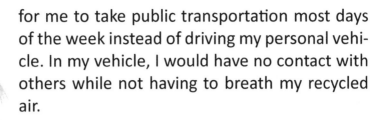

for me to take public transportation most days of the week instead of driving my personal vehicle. In my vehicle, I would have no contact with others while not having to breath my recycled air.

Since the mandate doesn't start until Saturday, I'm happy to know in five days this virus will be more deadly on the bus. If masks work, why are they waiting? Like Steve says, "You can't fix stupid!"

The humidity here is so thick it restricts my airflow with a mask. That along with packing me on a hot bus between people would be enough to push me over the edge.

I feel sorry for the people who have to get out and are being forced to travel this way.

Borders are Opening
June 26, 2020

100 days self-isolating.

I just opened an email from the U.S. Embassy San Jose. Costa Rica borders are opening on August 1, 2020.

According to the U.S. Embassy, "Minister of Health Salas stated that as of August 1, foreigners from countries that have "controlled the spread of the Coronavirus" will be allowed to enter."

At this time Costa Rica has not announced what countries are going to be allowed in, however, it sounds like the EU and Canada will have a good chance of making the cut, but at this time no one knows. What we do know is the United States has a high likelihood of not making this list since the number of infected is one of the highest and still rising.

Scorpion
June 27, 2020

Well, it happened! After 5 years with no stings, today was my unlucky day. The attack happened during my morning shower when reaching for the bottle of soap. I wish I could tell you it was in the outside shower, but this happened inside.

People have told me it's like being stung by a bee. Now, I have been stung by many bees over the decades. The worst was a group of killer bees that got me under my eye and a couple stings on my hands. So, I know what kind of punch these flying creatures can pack.

I can see why people say it's like a bee sting because it happens quickly and it's a stinging feeling. But I'm not kidding you the sting of my predator was 10 times worse than a bee. Still not sure what had stung me, but aware it was running around my bare feet now.

My screams rang out and became even louder as the soap got in my eyes. I try not to fall through the glass of the shower door. I danced around on the wet floor of the small shower trying to avoid my attacker. Still screaming from the pain, I found myself backed into the corner. As my eyes came back into focus, I recog-

nized the arachnid when it stopped running and took a stinging position with his tail. This was about when Steve had made his way from the other cabina after hearing my screams.

He was just in time to witness what was left of the war. "Scorpion!" I yelled as I grabbed the conditioner bottle that was above my head. Swinging it down as hard as humanly possible not just once or twice it was on the fourth, or fifth hit that I finally heard his voice asking if I was ok?

Sitting naked on the shower floor looking up at him with tears coming down my face all I could say was "NO I'm not ok"!

Maybe it's because the sting really hurt. Or maybe it's because we have been in lock-down for 96 days and things that normally don't bother me are now starting to. Things like my husband seeing me have a weak moment. For whatever reason I feel defeated, and the flood gates have opened. Now is as good of time as any to have a good cry.

Bugs and creepy crawly things like snakes and tarantulas are much more likely in Marbella than Tamarindo or even Langosta. I was aware of this before the move, but was I prepared? This will be the 15th scorpion in seven days. The increase in scorpions happened this time last year as well. The locals tell me it's the change of seasons. We have tried every home remedy from plants to oils to keep them away and nothing seems to work.

This is why I always have Benadryl on hand. Even with the medication, my hand hurt for 3 days.

Tip: Fuzzy pet lovers talk to your vet. Ours told us a couple of different pills to have on hand for stings and snake bites that are common in our area.

Blue Passport No Longer GOLD!
June 28, 2020

Not Everyone is Welcome!

They just announced what counties will be allowed in when borders open on August 1, 2020, after being closed for 136 days the county will open back up. But NOT to everyone including the U.S. This is a very sad night in the Page house since none of the family can come to visit and if we leave, we can't come back.

Well, here we go again, a huge decision once again. Do I start liquidating everything or do I wait and see what happens? If I wait it could cost me even more.

This time five years ago we liquidated all our stuff down to a couple of suitcases so that we could move to the "Happiest Place in The World". This was the best decision we could have made as a family.

Over the last five years, we have lived a minimalist life-style. However, over the years some household furniture and a couple of vehicles have been added. This stuff will need to be sold if we are forced to leave the country.

So, What's the Problem

Here's the problem, my daughter and my U.S. passports have a visa stamp that reads "03 ENE 2020" with a handwritten 90 on the line. This visa stamp expired on April 2, 2020. Steve was on one of the last flights back before the borders closed so his stamp expired on June 15, 2020. The Costa Rica government has extended our visa until August 18, 2020, but that does not mean they will continue to do so.

This means we must leave the country on or before August 18. Normally, this would not be a problem. Usually, a quick trip to the Nicaragua or Panama border or even jumping a flight back to the states for a little vacation will take care of this. However, this approach is not an option. There is no quick border run this time.

Panama is Closed

Panama has closed its borders with no signs of opening. Nicaragua is not testing many. The canton that lines the Costa Rica and Nicaraguan border is now classified as an orange zone, which means it's HIGH RISK because of the high amount of people infected.

The government claims the zones are designed to minimize areas of high numbers of infected/exposed people from coming in contact with those in areas with low infection rates. I am not allowed to drive my personal vehicle into a different colored zone because the allowed license plate numbers are not the same between zones. A

license plate ending in "3" may be allowed on Mondays and Fridays in a yellow zone, but only on Tuesdays and Thursdays in an orange zone. None of the zones have the same days, so there is no way to cross zones with the same personal vehicle. The only way to get to the border would be through public transportation or renting a car.

Currently, these orange areas have more restrictions. Reports are showing that most of the infected are Nicaragua migrant workers who are here to help with the harvest.

With high numbers surrounding the border and little to no testing in Nicaragua to confirm their infection rates, the chances of this border opening are slim to none. I can cross over to Nicaragua, but I will not be allowed to come back into Costa Rica. As a result, these border runs are not an option.

Repatriation Flights

United Airlines has been doing repatriation flights for the last couple of months. At first, these flights were only every couple of weeks. They have increased flights weekly leaving Monday, Wednesday, and Friday. During June, Spirit Airlines also added a repatriation flight. All these flights are out of San Jose.

A big downside to these flights is that we would have to

fly out of San Jose. The city has more infected people than the beach towns, making us more at risk to encounter an infected person during our travels, and San Jose is not as close as Liberia where we usually fly out of.

It is 29 miles (47 km) from Tamarindo to the Liberia Airport, but 154 miles (247 km) from Tamarindo to the San Jose Airport. That is almost 5 times further! Plus, the extra 4-6 hours of drive time depending on road conditions.

Once again, I have been in self-isolation with little to no contact with the outside world for 102 days, avoiding the world so that I won't get sick. The thought of going somewhere with a higher number of infected people is just the opposite of what I want to do, but I might not have a choice if the government doesn't extend our visas. Without an extension, we will be forced to take one of these flights with no way to return.

Another major concern is flights home have been running four to six times more expensive than normal. While United and other airlines show new flights at cheaper rates, they all seem to be getting canceled so the only flight that would be worth booking would be one of the repatriation flights coordinated with the embassy which have lower cancellation rates.

Tickets Home are Expensive

A quick look today shows that a ticket home on one of these repatriation flights would run me $1,976.36 per person. The total for all three of us comes to a whopping $5,929.89! We also would have the added expense of traveling to San Jose instead of Liberia.

Normally we would drive our own car and park it for free at the Liberia airport or pay $25 a person for a shuttle from Tamarindo to the Liberia airport. Parking in the city is expensive and risky so for us it is not an option, and a shuttle is going to cost over $120 a person.

MileagePlus: Sign in or join

One-way (1 traveler)	Edit search
Wed, Jul 01, 2020 SJO - DEN 12:48 pm - 9:00 pm	Revise
Fare	$1,810.00
Taxes and fees	$166.36
TOTAL	**$1,976.36**

Repatriation Flights Have Been Filling up Quickly

As a result, traveling home this way will be very expensive. Normally, the flight to Colorado and transportation to the airport would cost me under $300 per person. A flight and transportation to the United States are now going to run me at least $2,096.36 per person.

We have three people that will require flight and transportation. In turn, what would normally cost me around $900 but for all of us to get home will cost me over $6,289.08.

Not to mention it will add an extra day of travel. These repatriation flights have been filling up quickly with prices skyrocketing as the flights approach full booking.

According to the announcement yesterday, it sounds like the Liberia airport has met the standards to open on August 1, 2020. This means we might be able to fly out of (LIR) but at this time flights are not guaranteed.

Keep in mind we can't drive most days, so a couple of nights of hotels next to an airport might have to be added. Also, many of these hotels have closed down creating additional logistic challenges.

Chica, you need to make up your mind! Do you give a 30-day notice and decide you have to go even if it's going to hit the pocketbook, but being stuck with rent and utilities next month for a place you can't even live in would

suck. Remember how much that pool pump costs and you won't even be able to use it, but you will pay for it!

However, at this time the Costa Rica government has only extended the visas until August 18, 2020. Since the land borders are closed and our visas have not been extended, we are left with only a couple of options.

Option 1, Fly back to our home country on a repatriation flight.

Option 2, We wait to see what the government does. I have to be a realist and ask myself how much it is worth to me. Knowing that August is just around the corner and if we are forced to leave, we will not be allowed back in until borders are open to the U.S. The reality of our return could be next year or even longer.

Going Back to the U.S.

While I would love to put my arms around my parents and children, the risks from travel and looking at the numbers of infected in the U.S. scares the hell out of me. However, if I wait to book a flight, I run a chance that they will cost even more than what they are now since all the expats who are here on tourist visas will have to fly out during the same small window with few available flights.

What about all our possessions? The fact is it's going to

be harder selling our stuff since everyone else will be doing the same thing. Heck, they are already. I've lost more expat friends in the last 2 weeks than all 5 years combined.

Everyone is going home!

It Only Takes 30 Days
June 29, 2020

Remember when they told us lock-down was only going to be 24 days. That was 103 days ago, and we are still in lock-down with no end in sight!

One of the things that I was well aware of before all of this started was 30 days is what it takes to develop a habit. By repeating an action consistently for 30 days it becomes routine. One thing is for sure I tried my best to keep the routine in place. But hey what can I say, I'm human and it has not just been days, it's been months.

Let's face it, the TV has now taken over my evenings. Most mornings are no longer greeted with the sun rise but more of the later morning. I have still made sure to write every day. The 90 day challenge I started with a group of marketers has now been over for almost two weeks. Let's face it this chica is tired and bored.

Looking back over the last couple weeks I don't even recognize myself. Daily habits no longer exist. I'm eating differently and even my mind set about everything has changed. I'm forming habits, bad ones.

JULY 2020

Summer School
July 2, 2020

Way to go Taya! Final grades for summer classes are in and are all A's! One thing is for sure, this young woman has done it again. Online learning was something that did not come easy for either of our kids who received the worst grades ever during their first year. As a parent, it was so hard to watch my children fail.

I remember long talks with my husband about this new way of learning that was difficult for them, but how long do we let our kids fail? Not only was it killing me as a parent to watch them struggle, but it was also costing us in the pocketbook because every "F" meant a child has to repeat a class that we had paid good money for.

To this day I remember his words clearly, "It's hard to do new things, give them time."

This mama was concerned, they were not going to graduate and summer school was a must for both of them that first year. However, that was all it took for both kids and after about 12 months they had learned what it takes to do online learning.

Summer school of 2020 Taya is on track to graduate with her class of 2021, but since travel is not an option and the

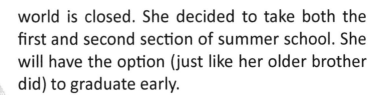

world is closed. She decided to take both the first and second section of summer school. She will have the option (just like her older brother did) to graduate early.

Way to go Taya while the rest of the world was watching TV you did something amazing!!!

Happy Independence Day to the USA!
July 4, 2020

I should be there right now but had to cancel my trip! What I would do for some fireworks. Even if I had made it home this year, Colorado is on fire and almost all firework celebrations have been canceled. As a matter of fact, this has been the worst year on record for wildfires.

My kids sent pictures and videos from dad's property during their evacuation. I could see the flames of the fires coming over the mountain ridge making their way down the other side. I wonder if there will be a farmhouse to come home to.

As if that was not enough, the pictures that I have been seeing over the weeks look more like Armageddon. The mountains burn out of control. Dark skies block out the day. It has become so dark that streetlights with light sensors stay on during the daytime.

The sky rains down ash that covers the state like snow. The air is filled with so much smoke my in-laws in the next town have to pull the batteries out of the firer detectors because they keep going off. The burning red sun shows it's faces through the dark clouds of smoke as it sits over the beautiful Rocky Mountains. It has made for some amazing photos, while leaving me with a creepy

end of days feeling.

Extra prayers for my family and friends back in CO.

Visa Only Extended
July 8, 2020

Great news, tourist visas have been extended! Foreigners who entered after December 17, 2019, can legally remain in Costa Rica until November 18, 2020. We can stay on our secluded jungle hill until the holidays. Hopefully the world will recover, and we can take a visit home for the holidays.

Just like last time, it looks like we won't be able to use our driver's license. The biggest issue is groceries. I don't mind the couple mile walk to and from the store, but let's face it, carrying things back is hard. Drinks, beans, rice, and produce are all heavy. This is slightly less of an issue because the store has not had much for fresh fruit since the trucks are not bringing deliveries. By the time we return home we are covered in mud from the dusty roads, 90% humidity, and sweat.

It's amazing how much the world has changed in the last 108 days. As I look back at my life, it is amazing how much I have changed.

Nothing Worth Doing is Easy
July 10, 2020

Work guilt is something that I have always struggled with as a mom. Remember you have a 17-year-old watching everything you're doing and it's ok for her to see you struggle while working long hours.

Keep this in mind, none of our kids were around during the writing of our first book. Even though Taya and Ellis were around for most of the taste testing of the cookbook they still were not around during the writing part.

I must remind myself, it's ok for her to see that it takes long hours from both Steve and me. I should not be ashamed of her observing this struggle because it is what it takes to write books while building and growing a corporation. It's good for her to see it takes hard work to achieve success.

Press Conference
July 23, 2020

127 Days of Isolation!

During the press conference, the government announced on August 1st, 2020, that Costa Rica would slowly start accepting international flights from countries that have "controlled the spread of the coronavirus".

It's no surprise the U.S. did not make this list since their number are so high. Like I said before I kind of expected it, but it does not make this any easier.

One thing is for sure over the months my Spanish is getting better. Even though I still can't speak a word, I can understand a lot of what they are saying during the press conference.

What's Dark and Scary?
July 28, 2020

Dark and scary is the Costa Rica jungle with no power and you can hear sheets of rain pounding the roof. Thunder shakes the walls and just as quick as the stunning light lit up the dark jungle, it was gone.

Capow! Crash! Snap! Boom!

Energy so powerful spiking through the air has this half asleep 5-foot 115 lb. body flying out of the hammock into a standing position. Every hair on my body is standing up! This chica has never felt energy and power so strong.

Sounds of screams are quickly drowned out by pounding rain. The pitch-black night set back in just as quickly as it was interrupted.

I rub my ears to stop the ringing of what just happened.

Quick assessment- I'm alive but the lantern that was used to get me outside shortly after the power went out was now nowhere to be found.

Faint screams from Taya could be heard but the words were drowned out before they could be deciphered.

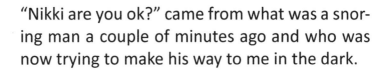

"Nikki are you ok?" came from what was a snoring man a couple of minutes ago and who was now trying to make his way to me in the dark.

Standing on my porch in what now feels like a cove. The water is flowing down the hill behind the house and wrapping around the sides. I was tucked tight between a waterfall of pounding water coming from all around me.

"I'm fine but I can't find the light. I'm pretty sure that was Taya's screams we heard across the property. She's ok, but the pool has been flooding for hours. Water is coming off the hill so fast between the houses I don't even know if it's safe to cross."

No stranger to the jungle storms, 2020 is going to leave its mark like none other. Tonight, was just the beginning of what I am anticipating to be one of the hardest rainy seasons of the jungle that I have ever experienced.

AUGUST 2020

Hobby vs Investment
August 5, 2020

I have been spending a lot of time writing this journal/diary/whatever this thing is. My use of time is coming into question. At the beginning of this pandemic, I was asked to keep an account of my experience as an expat. I am not sure if this will get published or not, but I see it as a good use of my time

When is a Project no Longer Considered a Hobby but an Investment?

This was the question in the board meeting today.

One of the responses was "when it makes money".

I don't agree with this. As a business not everything I do makes money. As an author, not everything I write makes money or even gets published. If I were a scientist, would my research only be considered an "investment" when my experiments are successful?

The average brand takes two to five years to build just like a new business. Most brands spend hundreds of thousands of dollars in brand development and testing, not counting the countless hours of work that might never pay off. While many in the world would say this is a hobby, most entrepreneurs, CEOs, or developers do this with little to no return in the beginning.

It's only after these people make money when people around them recognize them as being successful and what they do for a living as a career. I have been spending quite a bit of time journaling. At this point I am unsure if my writing will be published or if it is just an exercise to maintain my sanity while improving my writing skills. Either way I see it as an investment that will pay off in the long run. If for no other reason, I have been exercising my writing skills and my brain.

Others may see this project as a waste of time or just a hobby. I still count this as work time. Is what you're doing during the lock-down a hobby, investment or just being lazy?

Just something to think about.

Make the Voices Stop
August 8, 2020

My world has been on lock-down for 143 days. Saying this is crazy is an understatement!

I must look like a crazy person talking to myself, but as a writer with dyslexia, the dictate microphone on my computer is used often. This is when I need to turn it all off and just write so I can get the voices out of my head!

Let's not forget the music. For me, it plays a huge role in the way I write. However, I only have a handful of songs on my favorite playlist, and they are about ready to drive Steve and Taya to a different kind of crazy!

Rules Don't Apply to Everyone!
August 12, 2020

I find it interesting that the government leaders and people with money, not only from my home country but around the world, seem to travel and take trips out to do normal activities that have been declared dangerous to the rest of us.

Over the last three months, I have sat back and watched as the world leaders do things that make me question everything that is going on. They are telling us that we must mask up and stay in place or shelter depending on the country you are talking about. However, it seems that these restrictions only apply to people who are not in government or have deep pockets.

Why is it safe for them but not for me? Better yet why do I have to wear this fucking face diaper?

If the higher-ups can take trips to the beach over holiday weekends, why can't the common people? More government officials and people with money have been caught having big parties while doing whatever they want without face masks even after telling their citizens to stay home because contact is dangerous.

The examples are endless in countries around the world!

All I can say is wow. I don't care if you are "out in the public eye", Chicago Mayor Lori Lightfoot. If this is as deadly as all of you want us to believe, why are you not taking caution to save other people's lives? I'm sure the rest of the world would like a haircut! *(Wong)* It must also not be as contagious to the leader of Costa Rica either, since as of today President Alvarado is being investigated after taking a vacation to the beach. Are you kidding me? *(Times et al.)*

During all of this, I was willing to make a sacrifice to keep myself and others safe!

While the majority of the country, including myself who has been in isolation for 147 days with little to no contact with the outside world spent the holiday weekend stuck at home, these people went on with life as usual. My mental and physical health has been affected by the actions of our governments. Yep, I said it! After decades of therapy to learn the red flags of things in my life, I can officially say I've been throwing red flags for months!

Just in the last day, red flags have been thrown at my marriage, weight gain, sleep, body pain, mental health, finances, etc. and these are just a few areas of my life!
Let me pose this question. How much is a day worth to you? For me it's everything. I'm no stranger to death. Losing my sister at 28 years old made me realize life was short, but having a doctor put a number on how long you

have to live is a whole different time clock. In my book a day is priceless, 147 days is like losing 10 years to me.

Tell me once again why I'm sitting at home while they come and go as they want. It seems that only people on the lower totem pole must follow these rules. The sad thing is it's happening all over the world.

I hope they enjoyed their beach vacation as we sat at home on lock-down not able to drive or watch the beach sunset, where I would normally do my physical therapy and never even encounter another person.

This is just like one of those stories Grandma Hay would tell me growing up. In the end, she would say, "if you ever see this happening, you better start getting scared." This is a sign the governments are taking too much power or maybe it is all a big conspiracy. I hate to say that, but stuff is just not adding up.

Left Out
August 18, 2020

Borders are opening to the U.S., but not everyone! I'm feeling very left out. It's great news for some. Costa Rica Borders will open on September 1, 2020, but only to some states. Currently, Colorado is still not on the list.

Starting on September 1, 2020, the following states will be allowed to enter: New York, New Jersey, New Hampshire, Maine, Vermont, Connecticut, Maryland, Virginia, and the District of Columbia. Only these states made the first cut.

As I sit here and look at the list, I don't think they went with states with low or controlled numbers like they said they were going to do. From what I have been hearing, New York has been a hot zone from the being with the highest numbers out of the gates. From the looks of it, they went with states that were clustered along the east coast.

Once again none of this makes sense at all. Not all U.S. citizens that have valid passports will be allowed either. At this time, you must show a valid state driver's license. Plus, insurance and tests are required.

Tonight, before I go to bed, I ponder why a country with

some of the lowest numbers around the world would open to only a handful of states with high infection rates.

Dropping out of 1st place for highest infected but holding strong at 4th place is New York. New Jersey also pulling a top spot falling into 8th place for the highest infected states. However, both states are killing it when it comes to deaths. New York is holding 1st place with New Jersey right behind in 2nd place.

It's like they think the infected are only the ones without driver's licenses in these states. By that logic, we will all be ok since all these tourists will be renting cars so they can cross the colored zones on their travels. Happy to know we are still a threat driving our own personal vehicle most days of the week.

While not being able to access these zones due to our license plate numbers. I remember when we were told this was to keep the numbers down while containing the parts of the country that had higher numbers.

Let's sit back and watch what happens to numbers. For me I'm not as worried about the numbers of sick. I don't think this is going anywhere as people start to come out numbers will most likely go higher. The death numbers, ages, and if they have preexisting conditions will be more of what I focus on.

What Day of the Week is it?
August 19, 2020

Typical Costa Rica morning guessing the day of the week. 99% sure today is either a Wednesday or Friday because the fruit truck just drove by for the first time in months. It is common for us to lose track of days due to our flexible schedules and "pura vida" life in paradise, but lately it seems especially usual.

Since the fruit truck is out for the first time in months, perhaps I should put on my walking shoes and check the mini super to see if they got some fresh produce in.

Charter Flights
August 23, 2020

How many of my friends would be interested in a charter flight going directly from Costa Rica to Denver CO in November or December? I'm looking at private flights and charter prices will depend on how many people, luggage, and animals.

It's shocking after some research these flights might be the way we start to travel. With enough others, I can book a charter flight for as cheap as a commercial flight. Especially if there is a lot of luggage or pets. I just need a lot of friends to book with me.

Costa Rica Saved My Life
August 24, 2020

Our move saved my life, but it still didn't take away the fact that I have a relentless disease. Some days are harder than others. However, the truth is every day is full of excruciating pain, numbness, and lately vision problems.

Every single day my body is fighting a war! I'm struggling to walk today with more pain than I have felt in years. I remind myself that today is just a day that I have to fight a little harder.

Over the years some of my battles have included long periods in wheelchairs and months in hospital beds.

The fact is, the battle is going to be hard, and in the end, I know MS has a high likelihood of winning. But not today, because this chica still has crap on her bucket list. Time to put on my big girl pants.

As a matter of fact, my bucket list has been added to!

Remember to continue to live every day like it's your last since tomorrow is not guaranteed for any of us.

Driver's License & Passports
August 25, 2020

Before we moved, we both had a couple of years left on our Colorado driver's license before renewal, but we decided to get them renewed early to give us an additional five years. We did this because we didn't want to have a time frame where one of us was required to be back in the states for renewal without the other.

Many states, including CO, will allow you to renew online. However, you're only allowed so many online renewals and we both needed to renew in person. It just made sense for all of us to go in and start with new ones.

Remember to order your license early because you are going to lose a month in the US mail. Trying to have things mailed to Costa Rica can be a challenge. It is possible to receive mail here, and we even talk about it in our other book. International mail is nothing I would want to mess with when sending important documents or anything time sensitive. To me, it is just best to avoid mail.

Timing is everything! Having a friend bring mail and stuff to Costa Rica or plan a trip back to pick it up is probably the easiest. Staying on top of these things can save you a lot of time and money in the long run.

I'm now sitting here five years later, and my license is expiring. Remember, all I needed to do was go online and order it, but this time they are requiring me to get an eye exam. Originally, I would have done this during my summer trip home. No big deal, the eye appointment in Costa Rica costs less than $10 and the doctor speaks English. I am only required to confirm that I have had an exam on the online renewal. If requested I may have to show proof of the exam.

Getting the license to me in Costa Rica has become quite a challenge with the borders closed.

Keep in mind currently, you need a Driver's license from one of the approved states along with a passport and other COVID related documentation to enter. I always recommend checking with your embassy for an update on what is required and who is allowed.

You can learn more about driving in the transportation section "Cut the Crap & Move to Costa Rica".

Passports

To board most international flights, the airlines require you to show a passport with at least six months remaining (this is an airline thing, it doesn't matter what the rule is for the country). Something that I found interesting is how easy the US embassy makes it to apply for

a passport when you are in Costa Rica. However, just like everything, this has become harder since the pandemic but is still possible.

I recommended that you have at least a year left on your passport. This will allow for crap like the world closing down.

Tip: Keep all your old passports if you buy property, open a corporation, or purchase a vehicle, most of these are linked to your passport numbers. When you get a new U.S. passport, that number changes. You'll need to provide the old passports and new passports when doing transactions in the future.

More Allowed
August 28, 2020

More U.S. States are Allowed

Starting September 15th, 2020, travelers coming from Colorado, Pennsylvania, and Massachusetts will be allowed to enter Costa Rica..

This is all crazy! I never thought having a driver's license from Colorado would make a difference in getting into a foreign country since I hold a U.S passport. Now they require two forms of government identification for traveling. More specific, it's not just your countries passport, but also the state you live in now plays a role in international travel.

Not only that, but only drivers are allowed in. At this point a valid state issued driver's license from allowed states is required. I believe this is an oversight by the government and anticipate it will be changed to a state issued identification card.

This is another first in history!

SEPTEMBER 2020

Only the Rich
September 1, 2020

They're coming! Today is the big day! Borders are open after 167 days! Costa Rica opens its borders to some U.S. passport holders through air travel. Requirements are strict and not everyone who holds a valued passport is allowed.

For those who are coming, they have reported expensive insurance added to this as well as testing. One friend reported driving 3 hours one way and paid $218 for the test. How much is paradise worth to you?

Like always, people were abusing the system by taking out only a couple of days of insurance and then staying for the full 90 days. Customs is now giving stamps based on insurance and your onward travel ticket must match your insurance.

Nasty words
September 4, 2020

Flashback to 2015, Airline Tickets are Booked!

WOW, the negativity and nasty words almost kept me from booking those tickets. The bucket list was long, and the dream was big. People told me I was crazy and had lost my mind. They told me we would fail and come running home.

Multiple people called me selfish to my face telling me I had not thought about how the move would affect our parents let alone the children. Others told me I was a horrible and selfish wife. Maybe I was. How does a good wife tell her husband to quit his job and walk away from everything he has worked for, followed by I love you but I'm going with or without you?

Having big dreams is one thing but making them come true is a whole different story. Here's to making dreams come true and not listening to the negativity and nasty words that many try to spew into our lives.

Five years later my bucket list for this country has only one more thing to check off.

Our family has grown in ways I never thought were possible. Over the last year, a new bucket list has been started. It's longer than the one I held in my hands five years ago. I'm praying Steve is up for the next adventure because I like it when he comes along.

To put a checkmark next to most of the things on this list, I will have to risk it all again. This scares the hell out of me. But I know for a fact if there is no risk and it's not scary, I'm not dreaming big enough.

How Many Times in Your Life Have you Flown on an Airplane?

September 5, 2020

Hats off to my friend George who had the highest number. "2,563 (I checked my records)"

It's like my friends are challenging me! No clue how many flights I've been on, I lost count after 75 but I'm going to start counting from now on.

My friend Dan commented:
"How about how many planes have you jumped out of at altitude?"

Jumping out of a perfectly working plane has been on the bucket list for over 20 years but it's about time to cross that one off when the world opens again.

Beginning of the End
September 7, 2020

Just another day in the "Cut the Crap" house. Hours of ad copy and design followed by hours of appealing every ad after Facebook rejects them. This has been a problem since publishing, but 99% of the time if I take the time to do an appeal the ad would be approved.

Little did I know that this was the beginning of the end. Over the last couple of weeks, all social media has blocked me for using the word "CRAP", causing me to lose some of my big accounts like Pinterest. Spending weeks in Face-book jail multiple times for using the word "crap" and even words like "travel" and "masks".

You know those days where you want to just pull the cov-ers over your head. Wishing the world would go away. Well, I'm having one of those days. In two hours, I have a board meeting I really don't want to attend. I have been laying here since last night trying to think of a solution. Just like the last two weeks I have nothing.

Kick me while I'm down! It's hard to grow a brand, even when it's a #1 brand, if no one can see it! We are going to have to re-brand this year or find another way to make money. The private platforms are now pushing us out if we don't conform or agree with them. How am I going to

tell Steve?

Book Signings are Off!

Don't forget, you still have not told him that all the money for the books that were sold to the bookstores will be returned next month. All the printing fees will be coming out of his royalty check since neither of us could do our appearances for the signings.

I guess this is the prices of doing business with the bigger bookstores. I was aware when we signed the contract if we did not show up the books would be destroyed. Let's be honest we had every intention of being there. By destroying the books, the stores will receive their money back from the printers. This practice is great for the bookstores, but someone must pay for the printing for the now destroyed books. One thing is for sure, it's not coming out of the printer's pocket; but the writer and publisher are on the hook.

My dad would tell me to work even harder to increase sales, but at this moment I don't know what to do! In less than 72 hours most avenues of book promotions have stopped. Just like every other business owner, I know who did not close down during the pandemic, my staff has been working more hours than normal just to keep up with the changes. Everyone around me is tired.

Now that we have mourned the money that was lost, it's time for this girl to think even more out of the box! Changing the title on the first two books is not an option. It would confuse my readers along with a whole list of

other problems. International travel and book signings are not going to happen for the foreseeable future, so what am I going to do?

Giving up is not an option!!!

What can you do to bring in more money if all lines have been cut off? It sounds like a question that we would ask in business training class; however, today I will ask this question to my publisher and board of directors. At this moment I have no back up plans as to what we should do. My guess is at the end of the meeting my board will vote in favor to conform by changing my brand name, and maybe even my first two book titles.

Heartbroken is what I feel after six years of testing and brand development. The thought of building a new brand for something that has been proven to be loved by many around the world just makes me sick to my stomach.

Today's meeting is going to suck! I might as well make a zoom meeting with Michele for wine. Thousands of miles might keep us apart, but a video chat brings best girl-friends together after a hard day. Hell, I might break out the drinks at the meeting because there's nothing like telling your partners they might not get paid next month unless we re-brand. I'm not talking on a zoom meeting to a bunch of idiots, they all know re-branding will take months if not years, not including the cost.

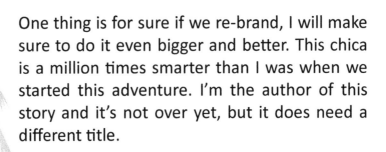

One thing is for sure if we re-brand, I will make sure to do it even bigger and better. This chica is a million times smarter than I was when we started this adventure. I'm the author of this story and it's not over yet, but it does need a different title.

What Driving Restrictions are About
September 8, 2020

Anger writing today!!!

After an extremely long day, I'm still pissed off. However, I did end up writing a blog about what outraged me.

But here's the thing....

It's not worth putting it in the book because it was more for my mental health to write it.

With that said, my dog did survive a snake bite only because Steve risked illegally driving to the Farmacia to save the animal's life. Of course, Titan got bit on a day we are not allowed to drive due to restrictions.

As far as driving in Costa Rica I give up! The dates and times for when a vehicle is allowed to circulate are constantly changing and even law enforcement can't tell me what is and isn't legal.

When I asked the Transitos what would happen if I took my dog to the vet, one informed me he would not take my plates while another said a sick dog is not a reason to break driving laws. He would have taken my plates and towed the car.

Guest Speaker
September 9, 2020

Crap! It's 6 am and the power is out. Plus, the battery backup for the Internet just died. Most days this would be no big deal, but today it's a huge deal. I'm the guest speaker at The Travel Collective today and the show records in a couple of hours.

Thank you, power gods, for kicking on just in time.

Check out my interview with April & Cindy from The Travel Collective. In the 7-minute interview, we discuss how we chose Costa Rica and our transition to expat living. It was great getting to share my experiences and thoughts with these fellow travelers. What are your travel plans now that the world is starting to reopen?

https://theultimatecostarica.com/the-travel-collective

Time to Shop?
September 10, 2020

My shopping partner is heading back to the states today. Safe travels Buffy! Shopping without you will not be the same. I'm even going to lose the four hours of outside contact that I had once a month.

Don't get me wrong I love my husband and child, but shopping is so much easier without them. Let's not even talk about the extra amount of money they spend when they are allowed to do the shopping. Yep, more chips and snack foods come into the house when they help. Hell let's be honest, it seems to be all that I have been buying nowadays. I can confirm this by getting on the scale or looking in the kitchen, not much fresh fruits.

It's Weighing On Me
September 11, 2020

The difference in the food here is life-changing. The weight we put on in the states is coming off finally.

I thought losing that weight in 2019 was hard, but how did she do it in the pandemic? I want to take a minute to say congratulations to Taya. The 10lb in 2019 was just the beginning and she has lost more than 60lb in the last year. In the meantime, this Chica has added 25lb to the scale.

Let's face it, time to come out of lock-down and get back into shape from food to exercise. It's also time to start letting friends in 'cuz being away from people is not mentally working anymore. It's time to start thinking about what those changes look like?

Not the Camera
September 12, 2020

Steve needs my help feeding today or maybe I need his help since it's my message box that has several questions about passports and driver's licenses lately. After the office meeting, Steve and I decided to record a video that talks about some of the things you need to keep in mind when traveling and relocating to Costa Rica.

This girl hates the camera, so this is something that I try to avoid as much as possible. Video cameras and live feed are a million times worse. To this day, I still don't know how Steve did a year of live feeds every day to grow our brand.

Happy Costa Rica Anniversary
September 15, 2020

It has been a crazy month in the Page household. Today we start what I call our biggest celebration since our move. This time five years ago I was on a flight to a country none of us had even visited. The dream was to become a Costa Rica expat. With another year checked off the decision to stay or go has been one of the hardest yet.

Leaving our older children, parents, grandparents, and friends was hard on all of us. The added struggles of a sick wife, two teenage kids in a country that we had never even visited while not being able to speak the language was overwhelming for Steve at times.

Steve, you're an amazing man for taking all of this on, I love you with all my heart.

While I can talk for hours about all the good in my life, I also have to talk about the bad. As I work on my next book, I'm trying to be as transparent as possible. This has been extremely hard for me to talk about my journey with Multiple Sclerosis and how sick I was or how my marriage was falling apart because neither of us could handle what was happening.

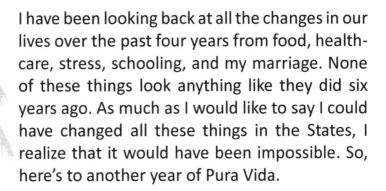

I have been looking back at all the changes in our lives over the past four years from food, health-care, stress, schooling, and my marriage. None of these things look anything like they did six years ago. As much as I would like to say I could have changed all these things in the States, I realize that it would have been impossible. So, here's to another year of Pura Vida.

I thank God every day that we took the chance. It's hard to believe we're starting our 5th year.

Reflecting on My Experience in Paradise
September 16, 2020

Reflecting on my experience, I offer a look into my first years as a Costa Rica expat. Shortly after moving to Costa Rica from the US, I learned about what some expats refer to as the one, two-, and five-year marks. These marks have come with many growing pains, lots of laughter, and new adventures.

As I look back at the past few years, I am not only impressed by all we have experienced and overcome, but I am also a bit shocked at how things have changed. I hope this glimpse into recent history will help you appreciate how much paradise has changed since the pandemic.

Making new Friends is Hard

I remember one night speaking with Taya who was 13 years old at the time. We had been here a little over six months. During this time, I had noticed she seemed to be having a hard time making friends.

We both expected this was due to the language barrier, however, she was also having problems with the English-speaking expats. One night I asked why she felt she was having problems and her response broke my heart.

She responded, "No matter how hard I try to make

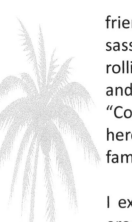

friends, all the kids say the same thing." In a sassy teen attitude and using air quotes, while rolling her head and eyes she imitated them, and the words came flying out of her mouth. "Come back and talk to us after you have been here for two years! You will understand if your family makes it that long!"

I expected many challenges when we considered moving, but not being accepted by our peers was not one of them. It is understandable now that I look back at how many of our friends have left and it has made me question if it's worth putting the effort into relationships as especially good friendships require investments from ourselves. Sometimes we can see these short-term relationships as a bad investment.

Why you Celebrate the Costa Rica One-Year Mark

After some girl talk that included tears, we made a pact that if we made it to these marks, we would celebrate them. We also agreed to never tell anyone they couldn't be part of our group because of the time they had spent here. Little did I know how big of a deal the one, two, and five-year marks were going to be.

One-Year Mark

Expat friends and fans who are reading this, make sure to take a day and celebrate this milestone. This one-year mark is a big day. **We lose about 50%** of the new expats during this year.

You have lived through Costa Rica's dry season, green season, and rainy season. By now you are aware that each of these seasons brings different challenges.

If you have made it through a whole year, you have most likely experienced the following: Culture shock is real and can be difficult to adjust to. You've given up on people showing up on time or even on the right day. If you are anything like me, you probably don't know the time or even the day of the week at this very moment.

Costa Rica Seasons

The seasons are different depending on what side of the continental divide you're on. Also, Costa Rica has micro-climates where the weather in small pockets throughout the country can change drastically. We have spent this last year on the Pacific side, in a small village called Marbella. I will use that as the reference point.

Costa Rica Dry Season

In February and March, winds descend from Lake Nicaragua. These winds affect beaches, cities, and mountains. No matter where I traveled in Costa Rica, I felt like the wind just followed me. Being sandblasted on a Costa Rica beach is not how I would describe a fun day. My friends that love to surf, however, will tell you this is their favorite time of year. On a good day, an offshore wind can create glassy tall waves that are super fun.

Honestly, its my least favorite time of year knowing that 60 mile-per-hour winds are blowing us into even more heat. April is generally hotter, but the upside is the winds are not as bad. This allows for more beach days and afternoons at the pool.

The months of hot winds with the temperature in the high 90's and even over 100 degrees can get old quickly but staying home and running the AC can get costly. If you live on the beach, you won't get a break on your budget during the dry season. Make sure to have an extra drink at your one-year celebration. I know how hard it is to turn that AC off because your budget might not allow you to run it full time, or the extra hours you might have to work to be able to afford over a $600 utility bill. It's enough to send people packing.

Costa Rica Green Season

Where do we start with the green season? One morning you wake up and the air is filled with even more humidity again. The flowers and trees all start to come to life. This happens right before the jungle rains start. Then slowly the Costa Rica rain showers start. The best way to describe this is the jungle springs back to life after a long hot summer. What you thought was a lot of green explodes into even more vibrant green. You can't even count how many different shades there are. If you took the time to acclimate during the dry season, this time of year can start to feel cool. We've acclimated to the hot temperatures of the dry season and now our family gets cold and starts pulling out our favorite socks and flannels.

This year our property had millions of lighting bugs. The jungle around the casa would light up in the dark jungle night. We spent hours at night laying in hammocks watching these amazing insects. Each morning greets us with new plant and animal life. You can literally sit on the porch and watch the trees and flowers as they bud out. Steve will tell you this time of year is his favorite, reminding him of spring in the US.

Living in a New World

But with all fairytales, you must wake up. For me, it was getting used to the creepy crawly bugs. They seem to show up even more during this time of year. Millipedes, beetles, tarantulas, scorpions, and black ants are just some of my unwanted house guests. This has been a big adjustment for me. We have more bugs in Marbella than we did in Langosta and Tamarindo.

A lot of our friends make the decision to go home during this time of year. By now most have spent around six

months here. What I call the holiday season is over. You know what I'm talking about. That really good vacation that you wish would last a lifetime, but towards the end, you can't wait to get back to your old surroundings. That feeling might have set in by now.

Culture Shock

Most people feel at least a sting of culture shock, which is compounded by missing family and familiar things. The rains can also affect some people. Many of our expat friends find themselves sailing right back to their home countries.

Missing my parents and kids was extra hard around the six-month mark. The separation added to the culture shock almost sent me home. Keep in mind that every-one experiences this at different times. I found it help-ful to keep a journal where I wrote the good and bad things down. For every bad, I had to find two good things. Keeping my bucket list as a reminder was ex-tremely helpful during my lonely times too. Calling and live chatting with my family and friends back home also helped. Thank goodness for modern technology!

Tip: As the rains start to come, so do more mosquitoes. Mosquitoes can carry deadly viruses called Chikungunya and Dengue. Make sure you bring plenty of bug spray from the states because it's expensive here.

Costa Rica Rainy Season

What can I say, this is my favorite time of year! This is what I look forward to during the hot dry months. These rains are not for the faint of heart. If you have experienced them, you know what I'm talking about. We love being stuck at home. I find these rains bring me inspiration, although most people don't like them.

Costa Rica rains start in May and June, but flooding becomes more apparent in August. What I call the real rainy season kicks in around September and increases even more in October.

We lose many new expat friends during this time of year. Maybe it's because they can't handle the torrential rains that can last for weeks or the muddy roads that can turn into rivers at a minute's notice. For me, it was the mold that almost pushed me over the edge. Yeah, I said mold. No matter how much you clean, it grows on everything.

Tip: Don't forget to pack a rain jacket. We prefer the packable ones, where they fit into their own pocket. This makes it easy to throw them in your backpack or beach bag for an outing.

Reflecting on the big day

As I wrap up writing this to you, I just spent the morning with no power because the rains and lightning took it out around 3 am. I know the time because the thunder shook the walls, as the flash of lightning filled the room, which was then followed by pitch dark, and the beeping sound of the emergency backup battery.

Rolling over I looked at the time on my phone remembering what I was doing at that exact time five years ago.

It was no normal Thursday morning. It was the last morning Steve & I would spend in the home that we owned for over 17 years!

We had a handful of hours until closing and this was the final asset that we had to sell to make this dream come true. It had been our kid's home since they were babies. Selling it and moving to a country 2400 miles away was scary.

Scared Gringo

Our flight was leaving in less than 24 hours, and I was mentally and physically exhausted. My anxiety was through the roof, but the bathroom had to be cleaned before the closing. Scrubbing the final room, I was asking myself If I had completely lost my mind!!! What in the world was I doing???

I was a scared gringo who had never spent more than 14 days out of my birth country. If I could go back and have a conversation with myself, it would look something like this.

"Anything worth doing should be scary or you're not dreaming big enough. You got this chica! Take it one coconut at a time. Be open to change. If life throws you crap, it's ok to change the dream. Just make sure that you check in with yourself making sure it's not just a distraction pulling you away from the dream.

Girl your dreams are big, but you can dream even bigger. You are capable of even more, DREAM BIGGER.

When you hit your milestones make sure to celebrate them. Even when others around you don't understand why. This is your journey, not theirs, so they don't need to understand."

Costa Rica Bucket List

Putting a check mark on my bucket list today. The "Cut the Crap" house will be celebrating our five-year mark all week. I want to take an extra minute to thank each and every one of you who has been part of our journey.

The messages, and words of encouragement along the way have been a blessing, as well as the friends who let me cry on their shoulders. Late-night calls to friends and

family who helped me stay on track were also beneficial. Thank you from the bottom of my heart. I could not have done it without all of you.

Pura Vida

To my parents and children, thank you for trying to understand why I needed to leave. To the love of my life, Steve, who risked it all for what some call his "crazy wife." I'm eternally grateful for what you gave up, so I could live this dream. The ride has been crazy at times, our adventures have been amazing, and I look forward to what the next year brings.

No More Minor Children
September 23, 2020

Happy Birthday to my youngest child Taya, you are now an adult. Yep, this is happening, your turning 18. It has been a crazy journey and I thank God every day for Him allowing me to be your mother. I can't wait to see how you touch the world as you spread your wings and fly.

Tonight, we decided to have friends over that have also been isolating for months. The night is filled with laughter and drinks, but the night is cut short due to driving restrictions so they must leave before 7:30.

Be thankful for your friends! It's has been over 200 days since we have had people over. If my memory serves me correctly, it was also George and Mindy at that time. We had taken in the local Fiesta a couple of weeks before Steve returned home, and then the world locked down.

The center of town that usually is filled with soccer games and even bull riding during Fiesta season has now overgrown with weeds and mother nature has reclaimed the ground that was going to hold new lights for evening games.

The yellow tape is still hanging from the new playground equipment that was installed right before the pandemic.

I don't even know if the kids have had a chance to play on it.

It was a great night! Happy Birthday Taya! Our evening is super enjoyable with drinks, great food, conversation, and a showing of the "Bucket List". All I can say is, it was really cool that our friends brought a movie projector to our home for movie night.

The bad news is the AC is not working due to a power surge that took out the motherboard. This is the second one that has been replaced in this brand-new house in the last year. The first one took over 30 days, to a tune of over $275.00. I can't imagine how long this one will take with all the technicians on lock-down.

Passing Notes
September 29, 2020

I watch as friends struggle with staying at home. Finding it very empowering as we all work together, trying to help one another. From work to home schooling kids or just being a friend to talk to after a long day of life. Let's face it, even the home body veteran who has been working online and had kids in online school for years is having a hard time with all of this.

Another day of life in lock-down around the world. Thankful for old friends as we chat between work, spouses, kids, and other day to day life. None of this would have been possible when I was young.

One of my favorite parts of school was passing notes between classes with my friends. The little pieces of paper were folded in different origami shapes and held valuable information. There was always some news that had to be shared from where we were going to sit at lunch to whom had a new crush that day. Better yet, what time I was going to pick everyone up for a night of cruising College Ave.

Notes were passed between class periods and put in lockers. As we got older, they were even left on car windows. Now don't get me wrong, I'm not from the cave ages. We had telephones back then, but most of my friend's parents had party lines. Making and receiving a phone call was almost impossible since you had to wait for a neighbor to get off the line. While big as bricks cell phones had no texting option. Not to mention only the rich owned them and none of my teen friends were well off at that time.

One of my best friend's parents had a private phone line, but her dad was always on it. I remember the teenage arguments when she would ask him why he was always tying up the phone with his computer. He would respond with statements like. "I'm working on the Internet. Some day you girls will thank us because it's going to change the world."

Nowadays, we all know what the Internet is. But back then, it was nothing but lines of letters and numbers. No pictures no message boxes, let alone search engines. Now I'm starting to age myself as I go on to tell you, the first websites had not even been created when some of these notes started being passed. Since the phone was not an option, passed notes is how a lot of our information was received.

In order to access this thing he referred to as the Internet it required tying up a phone line just to see the letters and numbers that made no sense to us. He could read this foreign language of what he referred to as code as he communicated to people around the world.

One thing is for sure he was right; it changed the world. I feel like I'm back in high school or even junior high as I sit here passing notes. Instead of origami shapes, the messages are being received, through the Internet from all over the world.

Thank you, to the incredible minds that thought so outside of the box. What was once someone's big dream is now how I send and receive pictures of our days. The lines of letters and numbers that once tied up the telephone line making us mad as teens, now make it so we can talk in real time from thousands of miles away.

The senders and receivers of these messages are still the same small group of people I passed notes to back in the day. We have all kept in touch over the decades. However, in the last couple of months I have found myself talking more throughout the day with my friends since everyone is working from home.

OCTOBER 2020

Protesters
October 2, 2020

Today's social media question: What's the word on protesters today? Has anyone been able to make it from Tamarindo to Santa Cruz?

Protesting is nothing new. In Costa Rica they block the streets with cars while waving signs. This is just something that we have grown accustomed to. Respect the people as they tell their government what they think from gas prices to paying high taxes or insurance they protest a lot here.

Very rarely do these protests get out of hand or people get hurt. The government respects the peoples' rights to be heard and usually in a couple of days (sometimes it can take weeks) both sides work it out and roads are open again.

That's not the case this year as protesters have taken to the streets for weeks with no end in sight. At this moment they are not burning things like in the U.S.

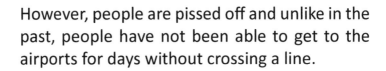

However, people are pissed off and unlike in the past, people have not been able to get to the airports for days without crossing a line.

Wonder how much more the people will take before things become violent.

Family Emergency
October 4, 2020

HELP: We have a family emergency and need to fly back to Colorado.

After receiving news that Steve's Grandpa past away last night, I sit at my computer pulling every bank account, and credit card that we have access to. I remind myself that money has been put away for emergency trips home, however, at this moment I'm questioning if we put enough away to get home in time.

I have always recommended when traveling that you have an emergency fund. How much to set aside depends on where you are going and what kind of travel accommodations you are willing to live with. While I know people who only have a little on hand or in an account, others have made sure that they could book a charter flight home just in case they needed to. These charter flights before lock-down ran about $10,000 - $25,000.

Never in my wildest dream would I have guessed I would sit here trying to figure out how to get home with so many obstacles. It sounds like it might take a boat and one if not two charter flights to make this happen.

Here are my travel questions today on social media:

Who is everyone using nowadays for private and charter flights?

Domestic flights?

I know flights are still being canceled. For those of you who have been able to get stateside what airport and airline did you use?

I understand the Costa Rica roadblocks are going to be a huge problem!

Can anyone tell me if flights are going out of Tamarindo to San Jose or Liberia? Is there a closer airport or landing strip to Marbella?

If I book a private or charter flight from Costa Rica to Colorado later this week who would like to buy a seat?

Who needs to fly animals back? I'm working on how much seats are going to cost, but I need a headcount and animal count first.

Since there are roadblocks with protesters both ways, here is how it looks so far. Steve can take a fishing boat out from the little village down the street. It sounds like they can take him to Tamarindo if the waves are not too big. Remember it's rainy season so storms could be a problem. From Tamarindo he can take a charter flight to Liberia. Where he can then fly stateside, that is if the flight does not get canceled.

Mandatory COVID-19 Insurance
October 5, 2020

Taking a deep breath before I look at how much the mandatory COVID-19 insurance is going to cost to come back. Steve has to go home to be with family. Our kids in the states can't have a funeral for Grandpa O without him. WOW! COVID-19 insurance is $1,900 for him and $2,296 if Taya joins him. Don't forget to add the $2,400 each for round-trip airline tickets, plus COVID testing at $100 each.

Grand total:
Steve $4,400
Steve & Taya $7,296

That's not taking in to account the boat ride or the charter flight from Tamarindo since the roads are still blocked. This trip makes the $700 round trip for the last funeral look cheap. At least that flight included seats and bag upgrades, not the back of the plane with no bags like these tickets.

These flights are expensive and have a high chance of cancellation. If I chose to do a big charter flight it would almost be cheaper and guarantee his travels. I just don't have time to arrange all the tickets sales or find around 200 of my close's friends who want to travel in the next three days.

I have always told Steve $10,000 should be more than enough to get all three of us home.

Note to self: Our emergency fund should be raised. I hate to see what next years living expenses are going to look like. No wonder so many expats are going home after months of not being able to get to their families the ones who now can travel can't afford to come back.

Voting
October 9, 2020

Have you VOTED yet?

It's time to vote. Today was exciting because we were able to show Taya how to cast an overseas/absentee ballot. The "Cut The Crap" house has voted, we challenge you to do the same.

Expats and overseas voters, it's time to vote. Four years ago, was the first time I voted using an overseas ballot. It might sound corny, but I missed putting my "I Voted" sticker on.

The first election I ever voted in was the 1992 presidential election between Democratic Governor Bill Clinton and President George H. W. Bush. Walking out of the little firehouse with the "I Voted" sticker displayed proudly on my chest, the excitement came over me. I was able to cast my U.S. vote today from my porch in Costa Rica. Voting in 2020 is easier than it was in 2016. The cool thing about voting this year was not even needing a printer or scanner.

19th Amendment

I find myself extra blessed that others fought for our rights to vote as women. This year marks 100 years since wom-

en could vote. Today I watched my youngest daughter cast her first ballot.

I know I have done my job right; Taya has her own opinions. Debating with both Steve and me on many of the amendments. Proud is an understatement as she backed her thoughts and feeling with facts. Even speculation on the good and bad that might happen if something was or was not to pass. I find it even more humbling as a mother to know Taya voted differently than me on some of the amendments.

This day we took a stand like so many other American women will over the next month and casted our votes. Something that was not possible to do 101 years ago because of our sex. Let our voices be heard.

Death is Hard
October 13, 2020

This is something that I never want to do again! After much debate about traveling, we decided it was just not worth the risk. Ticket prices and travel were high, but the reality was the chances of getting to the airport and having a flight in time was just not going to happen.

A big thanks goes out to our family and the funeral home who all bent over backward to include us in the celebration of life. Big thanks to our Internet providers for coming out and fixing the satellite that went out the night before during the storm. The service technicians jumped off the roof right as the funeral started.

I must give it to Steve and his sister Shawna. Thousands of miles might have kept them apart, but they were able to do a music video together! So thankful for technology! Amazing how it has been able to provide a little bit of peace during this time of suffering.

Invasion
October 15, 2020

Oh, Hell no!!

We are being invaded again. Our first invasion happened during dry season. As we were sitting on the porch one evening, we looked out over the rocks of the driveway. The ground appeared to be moving. It was kind of waving up and down.

It took a couple of seconds to realize that it wasn't the ground that was moving but actually millions of ants!

Like a scene out of a horror sci-fi movie, it happened out of nowhere swarming every inch of the property from the ground up. I'm not kidding you! It took less than a minute and both the inside and outside walls were covered.

Grabbing the jeep's keys, our painful screams echoed through the jungle as we quickly realized we were no match to this amazing insect. These little buggers' pack a punch when they bite and as if that was not enough, they also send out a scent when they are in danger. This scent tells the rest of their troops to attack.

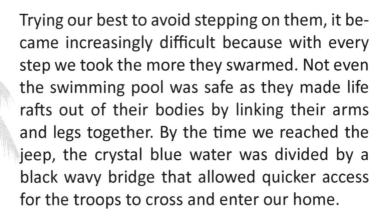

Trying our best to avoid stepping on them, it became increasingly difficult because with every step we took the more they swarmed. Not even the swimming pool was safe as they made life rafts out of their bodies by linking their arms and legs together. By the time we reached the jeep, the crystal blue water was divided by a black wavy bridge that allowed quicker access for the troops to cross and enter our home.

Black army ants are also known as "cleaner ants" here because they will clean your house. If you have spiders or any other insects, they will go through the nooks and crannies, and haul them off. The best part is, once they are done, they just leave!

We have had times where it can take anywhere between half an hour to several hours for them to complete their sweep and evacuate the area. They usually leave before nightfall, however, there was one occasion at the end of the dry season that the patrol stayed about an hour and a half past sundown.

Tip: Turn on the AC, they seem to not like the cold. It may not always stop them; however, it can help to keep them mostly on the outside.

Everyday cooking oil works great around door jams & windows. Ants don't like to cross the oil so just put a little on a cotton ball or Q-tip and run a line across the area. With that said, when the black ants come in swarms, there is no stopping them so it's best to pack up for a couple of

hours.

This experience happened quite a few times during the year and a half when we lived in Marbella but not once during the three years in Tamarindo/Langosta. In those areas the battle was more of the red army and little piss ants.

We try our hardest not to kill anything, however, if you must, Borax works great. You can get it at your local Farmacia. Then mix 75% sugar to 25% Borax together in a little dish. The top of a coke bottle works nice. Place in the area where the ants are. They will carry it back to their nests where it will kill the whole colony.

Note: there will be an increase of ants in the first 24 hours while they take the poison back to the nest.

You can check out my quick video of the amazing Black Cleaner Ants at the following link.

https://theultimatecostarica.com/costa-rica-black-army-ants

Big Day is Coming
October 19, 2020

Costa Rica announces that it will open-air travel to all United States passport holders starting November 1, 2020. There are still requirements and people who want to travel are going to have to pay for it to happen. From COVID insurance to testing the costs are rising.

After a quick search the airline prices are still high. But let's face it people who have been locked up in their homes for months are itching to get out. Can't forget all the people who canceled their trips and vacations.

The world seems to be split about staying in lock-down. It will be interesting to see how many of these people who have decided to come out will feel safe enough to do international travel. My guess is the vast majority, since people in my travel groups are already booking flights.

Seasons are Changing
October 20, 2020

Remember to embrace every minute! I'm sad watching the leaves fall from the trees. It's a sign that for Guanacaste rainy season is almost over, and the dry hot season is just around the corner.

The seasons are something that we struggle with since the months we like the most in Costa Rica are the months we like in Colorado too. One of the ways to fix this would be to move to the other side. The Caribbean side has just the opposite seasons of the Pacific side with many micro-climates to pick from. I like the vibe on the Pacific side as a whole, hence why we are on this side.

This time of year in the Gold Coast area is absolutely beautiful as the leaves change color before they fall to the ground. Bright flowers of all different shapes and sizes are everywhere. But if you blink you will miss it. Just as quickly as they bloom, they die. As the air starts to become hotter and the rains dry up.

The hot months are about ready to set in. For now, I will sit back and enjoy the beauty of my favorite time of year.

No More COVID Testing
October 22, 2020

Starting Oct 26, 2020, no more COVID-19 testing when coming to Costa Rica. This will save me over $100 a person. There might still be hope. However, I find this to be an interesting time to stop testing. Just something to think about dropping testing before allowing the masses in! In four days, they will stop testing, as air borders will open to all U.S. states a couple days later.

One of the benefits for the government is all these people will have insurance to cover them if they get sick. The downside is this is a small developing country. It would not take much to overwhelm the health care system, that has already been over worked and stretched to its limits.

I guess we will all sit back and see what happens to the numbers and how the country handles it. From letting everyone in to dropping testing, the Costa Rican government must feel it's safe to open back up.

NOVEMBER 2020

Welcome to Paradise
November 1, 2020

It was so cool to watch the airplanes land today! They used fire trucks and water tankers while the landing crew danced. The airport welcomed the first flights coming from the States after being locked out for 228 days.

Many families have not seen each other for months. I know husbands, wife's, parents, and children who will be reunited again. Homeowners that did not have residency will now be allowed to return to their properties.

I suspect the majority of these travelers to Costa Rica are property owners or have family here. The cost of travel is very expensive; not to mention, much of the world is still scared to travel.

This has been a hell of a ride. Remember when they told us it was only going to be 24 days. But I don't think this roller-coaster ride is over yet.

I wonder, did they happen to check the weather report?

Are You Ready?
November 3, 2020

Please stay safe everyone. As we buckle down for Hurricane Eta, the winds and rains have started, and power is flickering. Eta is now a major Category 4 hurricane but upgraded to a 5 in a couple of hours.

Here's what Steve has to say about storms Costa Rica:

Costa Rica tropical storms are no joke!

Situated 10° north of the equator and with 274 km (170 mi) of land separating the Caribbean Sea and the Pacific Ocean, Costa Rica is within striking distance of some of the most extreme storms on the planet. Surprisingly, few major storms make a direct impact or cause immense damage. In part, it's because Costa Ricans have always lived with the threat of tropical storms and flooding and in turn, they have adapted to their environment and are prepared.

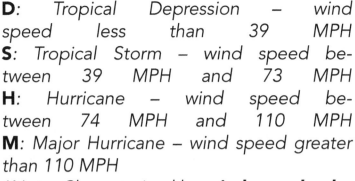

D: *Tropical Depression – wind speed less than 39 MPH*
S: *Tropical Storm – wind speed between 39 MPH and 73 MPH*
H: *Hurricane – wind speed between 74 MPH and 110 MPH*
M: *Major Hurricane – wind speed greater than 110 MPH*
Note: Characterized by **wind speed only.*

Costa Rica Recent Notable Storms

November 2020 - Hurricane Eta - Category 4 (non-direct)

October 2017 – Tropical Storm Nate - Category 1 (most costly)

November 2016 - Hurricane Otto - Category 3 (first hurricane on record)

Our Costa Rica Hurricane Experience

My family was able to experience the first hurricane on record to make landfall in Costa Rica. Hurricane Otto struck Costa Rica shortly after our 1st anniversary of moving to the country. We lived on the opposite coast, but we experienced a great deal of wind and rain. I remember huddling together near the center of our unit where there were few windows. The windows rattled and whistled from the wind, and the rain pelted the roof. It was very loud as the sounds flooded the room. Otto was an amazing storm.

As impressive as hurricane Otto was, it did not have the devastating effects of Tropical Storm Nate. The intense rains coming in from the Pacific dumped more water than many communities could withstand. It may not have had the wind-speed to categorize it as a hurricane, but Nate had plenty of power.

The thunderclouds released bombs of lightning and unleashed unrelenting torrential rain. We lived in Tamarindo, a very developed town with a strong tourist economy. The empty lots around our condo had several large trees washed out and blown down. We were without power for four days and had additional shorter outages in the following weeks. Hurricane Nate was the costliest natural disaster in Costa Rican history.

Flooding Happens Frequently and Quickly

Each micro-climate of Costa Rica experiences the rainy season. Depending on the region, rainfall can be as much as 440 mm (17.5 in) of rain per month. Floods are common, especially near creeks, rivers, or lowlands. Even quality homes can develop a leak, causing flooding during these times. Runoff and rising waters cause some homes to flood annually, whenever the strongest storms pass through. During the rainy season and certain tropical storms, *the rain remains constant for days to weeks in some areas. Without a reprieve, the limits of the rivers and creeks are tested.*

Costa Rica Roads & Bridges Washout

Roads and bridges frequently become impassible. When the water is too deep, you become cut off from food and supplies. Many rural areas have back roads that pass through a river that are dry or very low in

the dry season but become impassable when the rains pick up. Some communities have one access and as a result, may be isolated for days before the waters recede. If you live outside a city or enjoy exploring, you may want a 4-wheel drive vehicle. The roads can get rough and treacherous at times.

Another major event caused by flooding is mudslides. Many areas of Costa Rica are hilly and mountainous. Roads and lots are often carved out of the side of the hill, leaving steep edges. Saturated earth sloughs off, covering anything in its path below.

Costa Rica Lightning Storms can get intense

The rainy season can produce some strong thunderstorms. These storms can really pack a punch. The electricity flies through the air with frequent ground strikes and even assaulting the waters off the coast. It is only a matter of time before a strike is close enough to make you jump and your hair stands up

with the charge.

This discharge of energy is exhilarating but can cause some major issues with your electronics. Make sure you protect them. We have replaced a wide range of electronics from computers and TVs to musical instruments. We have had to contact repairmen twice for our air conditions. There is a voltage pro-tector for the AC unit that fails when overloaded. In our experience, electronics don't last as long, so you need to do what you can to protect them.

While scary and deadly, if struck, the odds of get-ting hit by lightning directly are slim. Lightning is the storm element we can most easily defend against and have the least chance of being physically harmed against, yet many fear it the most.

Costa Rica Wind, the invisible Force

The severity of many storms is measured by the intensity of the wind. Where precipitation and ex-treme temperatures can cause damage, the experts know to fear and respect the wind in full force.

Most of the time, the wind is more of a nuisance than a threat. But when it gathers its strength, wind can move great structures. Trees frequently lose their grip and fall. Often these fallen trees can be the cause

of power outages. The majority of electricity comes from overhead lines and when trees fall, they can take the lines with them.

The construction of many low-income houses in Costa Rica uses sheets of corrugated zinc for roofs. At times, these basic building supplies have been lifted off their nails and pushed like a sail through the air, exposing the living area or the residents to the elements.

Even the most well-built structures are not safe from the projectiles carried by the wind. Tree branches, garbage, and building supplies can crash through windows and damage the roofs. There is little one can do to defend against this invisible giant.

In the Guanacaste region in the north of Costa Rica, the wind can last for months. There is a current that travels down off Lake Nicaragua to the north and shoots out to the Gold Coast of Costa Rica. Vacationers of Tamarindo, Witches Rock, and Nosara experience the amazing surf created by the offshore wind to the Pacific Ocean.

Be Prepared and Keep Emergency Supplies Together

There are certain readiness activities and supplies we have learned to help us prepare for Costa Rica storms. Many are basic but the reminder always

helps.

Take a second to consider how prepared you are in each of these areas. Included are some links to some of our favorite readiness products that will help you be prepared during a Costa Rica storm.

Nothing is worse than having an emergency and not being able to find what you need. Hunting around for stuff in a power outage or minor flood increases your risk. Make sure the supplies are easy to access.

First Aid kit

Keep your First Aid kit stocked and accessible. Make sure you can grab it quickly, should you need to evacuate. We have a kit in the house and one in the Jeep that we use whenever we are on the go.

Extra Water

Often in a severe storm situation, the water can go out or can be contaminated. It is amazing how much water we use, including drinking, cleaning, and hygiene. We recommend having a large jug of water on hand at all times.

Fresh Foods can Spoil with Loss of Power

We cook with a lot of fresh local produce. If we lose

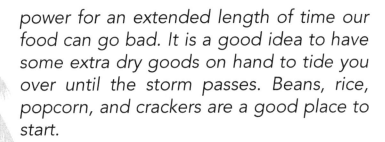

power for an extended length of time our food can go bad. It is a good idea to have some extra dry goods on hand to tide you over until the storm passes. Beans, rice, popcorn, and crackers are a good place to start.

Ensure Propane is Full

If you have a gas stove and you know a storm is coming, you may want to refill or exchange the tank. Being able to use the stove with the power off is a great asset. In the event your kitchen stove is electric, a Barbecue (Parrillada) is a good backup.

Coffee is a Must

Seriously, we function better with a comforting and stimulating cup of coffee. We have a Costa Rican coffee maker with a pour-over sock. If the power goes out (or the coffee maker breaks) we can simply heat water on the gas stove or grill and use the sock, coffee maker. This makes the best cup of coffee. These coffee makers also make great gifts.

Charge electronics & Portable Charger

When you hear a storm is on the way, be sure to get a full charge on your electronic devices. If the power goes out, you will need them for both safety and pastime. However, using electronics for en-

tertainment like Netflix can drain the battery that you may need as an emergency device. We use our electronics for news and communication which are essential in storm situations. Battery chargers are great to give you a boost if your running low. We strongly recommend getting battery backups. We have one on our Internet and for our other devices. Even if we lose power, we can still access the Internet. You can keep your computer powered and even recharge other devices.

Flashlights and Lanterns

Flashlights and lanterns are very underrated. I hear people respond often that they always use their cellphone as a flashlight. That is great for short periods, but what about when the power is out for hours or even days? Lanterns and flashlights can save the power on your phone for more safety and entertainment purposes. We highly recommend picking up a few lanterns and flashlights. We use ours very often. It works great to play cards or find things when the lights go out. Don't forget to keep a few extra batteries around.

Surge Protectors are a must

Any electronic device that you value highly should be connected through a surge pro-tector. Costa Rica is known to have many power surges and fluctuations. The poten-tial increases when there is a storm. Incon-sistent power is damaging to electronic components. Your devices will stop work-ing much sooner if you do not use a surge protector. Unplug your devices when they are not in use. This practice not only saves electricity, but it also keeps the device safe in an electrical storm.

The items listed above are also on my top items I pack. I hope these tips help you better prepare for your next storm and travel adventure. *(Page)*

You can find out more about the survival kit products I talk about at the following link:

https://theultimatecostarica.com/survival-kit

First Time Eating Out
November 4, 2020

While Hurricane Eta did not have a direct hit on Costa Rica it still brought lots of rain and flooding to the country. For us the storm was no different than a heavy night of rains. This afternoon the sun still has not shone however the rains have subsided a little. I want to venture out even though we are not allowed to drive today. I wonder if I could talk Steve and Taya into going out and getting a bite to eat?

This is something that doesn't happen often even when there is not a pandemic. As the country starts to come out of lock-down stores are beginning to open. The little restaurant outside the ferretería (hardware store) down the street that we have been walking by for months is now open. Whenever we walk by on our way to town the food smells delicious.

While I'm still not for sure how safe I feel about going out to eat. I have to be realistic with myself; how long am I willing to stay away from the world? I'm I going to live life in fear forever? Let's face it I don't want to stay away from the world anymore. Eating in a restaurant that is open air is as good of a place to start as any. Heck, my friends from the states have been having food delivered for months and so far, none of them have gotten sick.

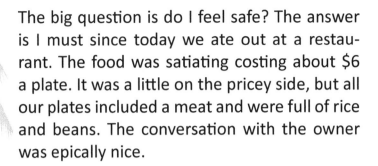

The big question is do I feel safe? The answer is I must since today we ate out at a restaurant. The food was satiating costing about $6 a plate. It was a little on the pricey side, but all our plates included a meat and were full of rice and beans. The conversation with the owner was epically nice.

There are many places where you can find $3.50 - $5 plates. One of the best plates I ever ate cost $4. It was also the freshest food I have ever had in my life. After I ordered my food, the lady stepped out and actually killed the chicken in the back of the restaurant. Talk about fresh!

Do you Feel Safe Traveling on an Airplane?

November 08, 2020

Over decades of traveling the world one thing that I can say for sure is getting sick when traveling is nothing new. Over the years I have learned that flying usually carries a higher risk of making me sick. Most of the time it's just a small cold like stuffy nose. I can blame this on breathing recycled air or just coming into contact with lots of people during my travels. Sometimes it's just jet lag or time change that throws my body off.

I could tell you I get sick more than other because of the autoimmune disease. But in all reality my friends and family members over the years seem to get sick as often as me when traveling. That is all of us except for Steve who almost never gets sick. Let's be honest getting sick is nothing new when it comes to travel; however, this is a worldwide pandemic and people are getting sick from breathing the air of others.

Can't Wait to fly Again

I just had a two-hour conversation, or maybe it was more of a debate about booking travel home with my stepmom Deb. All I can say is we are on different sides of the table on this one. While I understand that she is scared of us

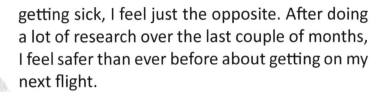

getting sick, I feel just the opposite. After doing a lot of research over the last couple of months, I feel safer than ever before about getting on my next flight.

While we were all locked in our home's airlines were getting better air filtration. If you don't believe me, check it out for yourself there are many studies and articles that have been published over the months. My favorite so far was a study done out of Harvard. "Flying During Pandemic Is Low-Risk, Harvard Researchers Say". [lanzito]. Maybe there is some positive out of all of this.

With better air on flights there just might be hope for all of us. Let's face it you're not going to live forever. I'm praying COVID is not what takes me out but hiding from the world is starting to be even more unhealthy than a 1% chance of death if I get infected.

Fly to Drive
November 09, 2020

This sucks, I just received an email from the Embassy. To legally drive you to have to leave and come back through air borders to receive a new stamp. Of course, to enter the country you must have valid COVID insurance. The question of the day is the government worried about people getting sick or is this about the money?

Telling people to travel international during a pandemic just so they can drive is leaving me scratching my head, am I missing something here? My guess it's all about the $$$$! Here's a thought, just let us pay for insurance.

We will just not drive. Leaving is not an option let's face it. I feel safe to travel on an airplane but, leaving and coming back during a global pandemic just for a stamp to drive is ridicules. My guess many will fly out losing their extended visas just so they can drive. Paying overpriced airline tickets and insurance to come back. The rest of us who sit, and wait are betting in the next couple weeks MOPS will take the side of immigration again.

Either way it doesn't matter Costa Rica, you can do better! Several months into a global pandemic and you should be able to get your government departments to work together. Its going to be sad to see what happens with the numbers as more people fly out and back in just so they can drive a couple days a week.

Nasty Election
November 11, 2020

Earlier I said this election was my easiest so far, that state-ment has changed over the past couple of weeks. 2020 was the hardest election I have ever voted in requiring assistance from an attorney to make sure that our votes were counted.

What can I say, it was a nasty election and very embar-rassing! We have turned all our news off for quite some time this chica couldn't take anymore.

Great! The soccer games or daytime Spanish soaps that once were shown in all the local stores, bars, and restau-rants have now been replaced with all the craziness that has been going on in the U.S. You don't even need to un-derstand Spanish to know what they are saying. For the first time in history, I'm embarrassed to say where I'm from and have no answers when they ask what I think about it.

I don't care what side you are on, both sides look ridicu-lous even on Spanish news.

A Chill in the Air
November 12, 2020

Freezing! You know it's cold when every layer of your warm clothing is put on with no regard to matching or style. Living in the tropics I don't own many warm items. I should probably also note that I have acclimated to the tropical climate and therefore the 21ºC (70ºF) feels extremely chilly to me!

Not only is it cold, but nothing has been dry for weeks. It has rained every day for weeks with little to no sunshine most day. Even the clothing that I pull right out of the dryer turns damp before I can even fold them! I know this is part of the rainy season, but today marks the fourth day of me being sick. I'm 99% sure it's not COVID, just a bad cold while my sinuses go crazy. The green NyQuil I brought from the states since I can't find it in Costa Rica seem to be keeping me alive right now.

I guess I will wrap up in my cold soppy blanket and embrace the dreary weather. But first, I have to do a live video with Steve about storms and Costa Rica weather. Of course, this must be done now since we have a feeling power is going to go out. This is going to be fun with the wonderful NyQuil high I'm on. Let's be honest people are asking in the groups for tips and how to stay safe. A live feed will be the quick way to get the information out.

It Does Not Take a Hurricane
November 15, 2020

Rainy days and nights are something that Steve and I look forward to during the hot seasons. Over the years November does not seem to have as many rainy days as October however when it does rain the storms seem to be more intense.

As predicted the power went out shortly after our live feed. No big deal, we'll settle in with candlelight for the evening. Shortly after the sun went down so did the Page household. Currently, the rains are nothing more than a normal rainy night.

(A few hours later...)
Nothing like waking up from a cold med-induced coma to the sounds of gushing water in the dark. The powerful thunder that had been shacking the walls was now being drowned out. Trying to get my bearings as I feel around for my phone that would allow me some light.

Dark would be an understatement pitch black is more like it. Have you ever been on a cave tour where they turn off the lights to show you how dark it can get? Well, I'm in the cave right now and I can't see my hand in front of my face. Let alone my cell phone as my hands feel around the bed where I remember I last laid it.

The intensity of the rain increases as it pummels the roof. But that's not what's concerning to me. The sound of rushing water like a river is what has my attention. This was one of the nights I wish Steve and Taya had stayed in the main house and not gone back to their own cabinas.

The property has a main house and two small cabinas that are separated by a pool. The structures sit about halfway up a big hill, backing to a dirt wall. The property had been carved out of the mountain side that lead to the top of the hill above. Our front porch looks down a cliff onto a dirt road.

The property across the street has a small creek that runs through the middle of it. During this time of year, it's hard to see since the jungle is so thick. This will be the second year in this home and our fifth rainy season. So, the rains are nothing new to us.

One thing is for sure I have never heard this much water running on all four sides of me. Using the light from my phone I make my way around the house. Quickly, I realized the house was working as a barrier between me and the flowing water.

The concrete walls redirect the waterfall that is pouring down from the mountain on the back part of the house. Sending the steam of water into opposite directions. Just before it's descent down to the next tier where it will join

up again at the bottom.

From what I could tell there was at least half a foot of fast-flowing water on both sides of the house. But none of the water was coming in. Realizing that my phone light was not enough to see outside. I grab the lantern however that did not prove to be much better.

Between the pitch dark of night and rushing waters, it was very apparent that crossing might not be safe. As I tried my hardest to see if Steve and Taya's rooms looked like they were underwater. Feeling paralyzed with fear I pray for the rains to stop.

The roaring thunder continues to be drowned out as the water pounds. Flashes of lightning gave a quick glimpse of jungles that were now being swallowed by the rains. Between flashes, I could see the little river across the street has broken its banks consuming the dirt road below.

Gaining power as it joins the waterfall coming from our hill. I find myself not wanting to get too close to the edge as I walk out onto the porch. But I need to see how high the flowing water is. I have seen homes higher up than ours washed away by the jungle rains in a matter of minutes.

We have a four-wheel-drive but let's face it, the road is now a river that is being fed from all sides including our

driveway. Since we have not been in the jungle building an ark, I realize there is no way out but on foot. Like I said it did not look safe but I'm sure I could get to the other side if I had to.

Did you bring a life jacket? Once again 2020 you are proving to be a challenge. Looking at all the possible ways to get my family out of the danger zone. I realize we have two life jackets in Steve's cabina that might keep two of us from drowning.

But in reality, there was nowhere to go. Trying to get down the driveway or through the lot next to us only leads to the road that was now a river. At this moment there was nothing to do but sit and wait.

Praying that ground around us does not give away to a mudslide. While the house continues to direct the flowing water around me. I spend the rest of the night walking the house every 20 minutes to make sure there was no water coming in. Writing by candlelight between the checks I find myself blessed that the water never breached the concrete.

What a heck of a storm as the sun is starting to shine. Steve joins me for coffee. Just in time to finish watching the running waters recede back to their banks. He informs me that there was not a drop of water in his room, but the back part of the cabinas have a lot of mud pushed against them.

We have a day of clean up ahead of us, but not until we have more coffee.

Patience Comes to Those Who Wait
November 16, 2020

Update, like always the transportation department is thinking about changing their mind about making people leave in order to drive. Sad for the people who flew out and back in just to be able to legally drive. Many of these people have been trying to avoid travel and big groups of people for months so they would not get sick. I guess the upside for the country is, they all must have specific COVID insurance in order to come back, so when they all get sick they can pay the quarantine costs and hospital bills.

Note: Some people who are getting sick have reported that the insurance coverage is not enough, and when hospitalized are still paying some out of pocket.

For me I guess it really doesn't matter since my U.S. driver's license was lost in snail mail. I keep praying it will show up since friends in the states are reporting to me that mail is taking forever. However, it has been months, so the chances are slim. My last email from them said that I would need to go into a local office in order to apply for another one. It's sad to say but if I want to drive again, I will have to fly back to Colorado. The upside is that Steve drives most of the time anyways.

Big Stages
November 22, 2020

As time passes, I am becoming more aware of the things that I am missing out on while we are forced to social distance. Today's "thing" is about my personal development. What I would give to hangout or speak at a conference right now.

I miss the big stages, classes, and mostly the people. Speaking and teaching at conferences was something I loved to do. It's hard to see the effects all of this is having on my friends who do this for a living.

Many are doing online conferences, and as a matter of fact, I have attended quite a few this year. I know how much work went into a successful conference before the pandemic. I also know how hard it is to get people to show up on a computer. It is extremely hard to get and keep their attention with kids and partners now in their workspace and personal space. I want to say "WAY TO GO" to all the people who pulled something like this off in 2020.

An extra thanks to Rachel Hollis and her team at Thrive. You all helped keep me on track during this time from moving my body to amazing conferences and my most favorite, your podcasts during my morning cup of coffee.

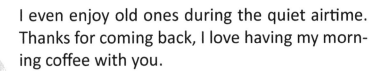

I even enjoy old ones during the quiet airtime. Thanks for coming back, I love having my morning coffee with you.

Let's call it what it is. This is the best alternative at this time, but it's not the same.

DECEMBER 2020

Taya is Going Home
December 2, 2020

First International Solo Trip Since the World Lock-Down.

Taya, you're amazing! I wish I had been as brave as you when I was young. This trip will be her second time traveling abroad solo, but her first since the pandemic. The summer trip she planned back to the states was canceled. Now, she will finally get stateside.

Over the years, my family has flown a couple of dozen trips back to the U.S. from the Liberia Costa Rica (LIR) airport. Most of these trips were to Denver International Airport (DEN) and cost around $225-$325 when I'm not using my credit card miles.

Expensive Tickets Home

In 5 years of traveling back and forth, these tickets are the most expensive tickets for main cabin seats I have ever bought. The same flight that cost $222 last year is now costing me over $600 more in 2020.

Keep in mind that the ticket did not even include a blocked open seat next to her like some airlines are offering during this time of social distancing. What was included was a direct flight from Liberia, Costa Rica (LIR) to

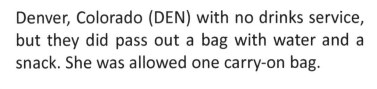

Denver, Colorado (DEN) with no drinks service, but they did pass out a bag with water and a snack. She was allowed one carry-on bag.

There is an upside to all of this. While still expensive, airline tickets have started coming down over the last couple of months. The ticket we are purchasing for Taya would have cost over $1,500 last month.

Airlines like Delta are blocking seats in parts of the aircraft. This means in some cabin sections they are keeping a middle seat unoccupied. One of the tickets I had been watching has dropped a couple hundred dollars making it $50 less than the direct fight, but the travel time is twice as long because of the layover.

Keep in mind that you are paying extra for most of these airline companies to offer to keep seats empty compared to other airlines that are not blocking out seats. In this case, I paid more for Taya to fly United to avoid layovers. The flight was almost empty 24 hours before take-off; however, it ended up being a full flight.

If you are a little more flexible, I have seen some flights from Liberia to Denver from $176 to $345 on Skyscanner. The downside to most of these flights is that they all have one to three layovers. Travel time is 9-31 hours compared to a direct flight that takes five and a half hours.

Do You Feel it is Safe to travel?

One of the first questions every traveler should ask themselves is, do I feel safe traveling? If the answer is yes, then ask yourself how much room you will need to feel safe during your air travels?

Is having a direct international airline flight with no layovers worth paying more money than layovers that add extra travel time? More airports mean more people and more potential exposure just something to consider.

We are choosing to minimize Taya's exposure and travel time. The layovers for most flights are in areas with high infection rates. The thought of her passing through customs and crossing highly populated terminals during high travel season makes me apprehensive. We feel much safer limiting her exposure with a straight flight.

Costa Rica is taking air travel and COVID seriously while requiring masks and social distancing. Liberia airport has also marked off seating to keep people safe during their air travels. In contrast, I have heard reports of some U.S. airports having minimal precautions in place. Maybe it's because they know everyone is going to be packed like sardines after boarding so why block off seats?

IN ADDITION, MASKS WITH ANY TYPE OF VENT OR FILTER are not allowed. We purchased the white mask at the local farmacia for 1,200 colones.

Safe travels Taya, hopefully we will visit you stateside soon.

Graduating High School as an Expat
December 18, 2020

Learning to adapt is a must as an expat teenager. What do you do when your trip stateside gets canceled? This was the exact question Taya found herself answering in April 2020 when her trip was canceled indefinitely. Graduating High School as a Costa Rica Expat did not go as expected, but this amazing young woman pulled it off.

Setting Goals to Graduate

Instead of letting her ruined plans get her down, Taya set a goal to graduate early from high school. She enrolled in both sessions of online summer school. Straight A's was also on the list. If she accomplished these goals, she would head from Costa Rica back to the U.S. over the holidays, assuming air travel is allowed.

Taking Advantage of Opportunities

While her friends and peers were wasting time in quarantine playing video games and watching Netflix, Taya took advantage of the time. She worked along side Steve to learn how to create products for the "Cut the Crap" line.

This mom got to sit back and watch as it took little time for her to take over the reins. Some of the items she has created are flip flops, bathing suits, holiday mugs and towels .

Finding a passion for something that she had never even thought about, Tays now has gone on to create her own custom line, "TPd - Taya Page designs". Way to go kid, you are AMAZING!

You can check out some of Taya's creations here: http://vivapurpose.com/tpd/

Costa Rica 2020 was a great year
Her year looked nothing like she had thought it would, but one thing is for sure, she did it. The summer credits gave her the equivalent of more than a semester's worth of credits. Taya graduated on December 18, 2020. As for those A's...way to go girl, you did it. All your hard work paid off! I can't wait to see what you decide to do next!

Testing & Quarantining After International Travels
At this time, Colorado is not requiring travelers to be tested or even quarantine; however, as a family we decided that Taya will be spending two weeks in quarantine. During these 14 days, she will finish her finals.

Over the years we have learned that graduation day is different since we do school online. There is no walking with your class to receive your diploma or big parties with friends, but no student should have to spend this special day alone. As a mother, I am disappointed that I am not there to hug her or eat a piece of celebratory cake, but I understand that she had to leave early so that she could be around the family on Christmas.

You are Good Enough for the Window
December 13, 2020

I was over the moon when a fan sent a picture of my book in the window of Esquina Del Souvenir Shop. This is my favorite souvenir shop in Tamarindo.

Never in my wildest dreams did I think thousands of people around the world would read my work let alone be good enough for the front window of stores. When we set out to write "Cut The Crap & Move To Costa Rica" we had a big goal in mind that was to help people.

Now telling you that numbers of books sold, and royalties checks are no big deal would be a lie; however, this took back burner to making sure that the right people got our product. This was so important to me since the whole point of writing the book was to help people. So, getting the book into the right people's hands was key.

Being humble, I'm married to one of the most humble men I know. As a matter of fact, he is just the opposite of me most of the time. Never wanting to be the center of attention and struggling to even put the #1 Best Seller on our titles because he believes it's bragging.

Over the years we have struggled with this part of our business. I see it as not bragging or even being prideful.

This accomplishment is something that we both worked hard for. Countless hours of work over many years. To me celebrating these milestones is important in reminding me that we are on the right track in helping others.

Making it harder for people to even find our books as platforms around the world ban me from running ads because of the obscene word "Crap". Today I do an extra happy dance to see my book in the front window of a popular souvenir shop. Knowing that not everyone in the world is offended by my words. For those who are, all I can say is just keep scrolling. My books are probably not for you.

If you are in the Tamarindo area stop into Esquina Del Souvenir Shop and say hi to Nadereh Tadjik. She has awesome souvenirs plus beautiful clothing, and essential oils.

No No No, Not Construction!
December 20, 2020

Why does construction always follow us? Better yet, why do they always break ground right after I commit to a publishing deadline for a book?

Our home office of our last condo in Tamarindo was ruined by the constant sound of grinders. Not only do we need relative quiet to focus when writing, we also record training videos and have live online classes. It is impossible to produce quality work with the sound of construction in the background.

The project that should have taken a few months took over a year to complete. During that time we had several instances where the power or water were shut off due to the construction. Needless to say, these issues made it impossible for us to work from home.

Now the secluded jungle home with the beautiful porch office space will be ruined. The amazing views and sounds of the jungle will be replaced by piles of construction materials, hammers, and power tools. And if that wasn't enough, the dust will make my office a complete sandbox.

The upside to all of this is we must get a 90-day visa stamp soon anyway. At this moment air travel is the only way to get stamped, so I'm booking a working vacation back to the states.

Excited is an understatement since my June trip was canceled.

It's been years since both Steve, and I have been to our hometown at the same time. Watch out Colorado, the Pages are coming!

Holidays Just Don't Feel the Same
December 23, 2020

Two days to Christmas and I'm hanging out on my porch while Steve soaks up rays in the pool. The palm trees sway in the distance as the monkeys yell at each other across the hills of the jungle. I love it, but it sure doesn't feel like Christmas.

Put on any Hallmark Christmas special or watch your favorite Christmas classic and you will see the standard markings of the holidays. You'll see images of fireplaces with cups of hot chocolate and snowball fights with scarves and mittens.

The stores are covered with decorations and filled with shoppers. You won't find much of that here. Few businesses decorate and not nearly at the level of the United States. Shopping may increase a bit but, in most areas, you won't notice much difference unless you are in the big city.

It can be difficult to get in the holiday spirit without the traditional commercialized version we have been immersed in when living in the north. What remains is the spirit of Christmas and the holidays. Kindness, Love, Generosity, these are the characteristics of the holidays.

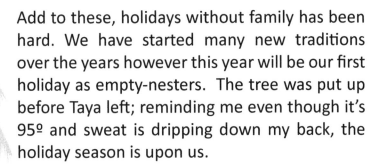

Add to these, holidays without family has been hard. We have started many new traditions over the years however this year will be our first holiday as empty-nesters. The tree was put up before Taya left; reminding me even though it's 95º and sweat is dripping down my back, the holiday season is upon us.

So as Christmas draws near, I will grab my cold beverage, lay back in my hammock, watch colorful leaves fall from the Costa Rica trees, and consider the kindness, love, and generosity that I experienced this past year and plan how to pay it forward into the new year.

Is Saving $400 Worth it?
December 28, 2020

Question of the day, is saving $400 worth the risk:

As I look for Steve and my tickets home, I find myself in a dilemma. Do we book the airline tickets with 2 different airlines and a layover at Los Angeles LAX or pay an extra $400 to avoid California plus have a middle seat open?

The penny-pinching side of me is having a hard time paying the extra for the tickets. However, my travel brain is saying due to high infection rates LAX could be closed in February. On the other hand, the more expensive direct flight is only flying at half capacity.

For me, before COVID this was a no-brainer you pocket the money and take the cheap flight; however, traveling has changed so much.

What would you do? I was asking this question on social media while I booked our tickets today. The response was pretty much what I expected, the majority of people said avoid California at all costs "it's priceless".

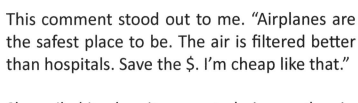

This comment stood out to me. "Airplanes are the safest place to be. The air is filtered better than hospitals. Save the $. I'm cheap like that."

She nailed it when it comes to being on the airplanes. Yep, I feel safer traveling now than ever before because of the new air filtration systems. However, I don't feel safe going through California. I am not sure if I am more afraid getting sick or simply being imprisoned in quarantine.

I just bought tickets home for February while Steve just confirmed the seats will allow both support dogs since checking them in is not an option through the airline anymore. As a matter of fact, flying furry friends has become way harder since the government changed the law about emotional support dogs and most airlines are not allowing animals in cargo anymore.

Once thing is for sure I'm nervous about flying with the dogs, even though we have been training them for months knowing there would be a day they would fly. Both are doing great with their harnesses and commands. At this point I am pretty sure I need more training than them. But let's face it, just like us they have not been around people.

Happy New Year
December 31, 2020

Happy New Year, but that is not all that we are celebrating today. Tonight, at midnight Steve and I will celebrate our 22-wedding anniversary. Plus, we will celebrate our best year in the publishing business.

Taking most of what was on my vision board for 2020 and relocate it to 2021, I ask myself if I'm being realistic on the travel part of next year. Since 2020 was a year of canceled travel around the world, my guess is 2021 will look much of the same, but that is not going to stop me from dreaming. Obviously, travel is going on my vision board. It's going to hit the pocketbook, but I can come and go from Costa Rica right now. As of today, many other countries border remain locked down to U.S. passport holder.

Over the years I have lived vicariously through my husband Steve who he has been able to travel and work in all three of my dream countries Greece, France, and Italy. I question if these counties are going to require vaccination before entering? Since I'm a betting woman, my money is on yes. The next question is will they require quarantine after entering like so many other counties? It does not matter because all three will go on my vision board.

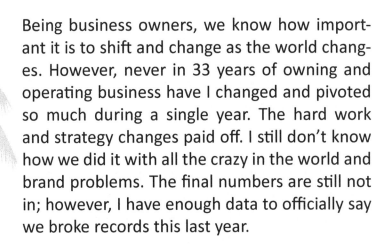

Being business owners, we know how important it is to shift and change as the world changes. However, never in 33 years of owning and operating business have I changed and pivoted so much during a single year. The hard work and strategy changes paid off. I still don't know how we did it with all the crazy in the world and brand problems. The final numbers are still not in; however, I have enough data to officially say we broke records this last year.

To start 2021, I will work with my team to re-brand so that we are compliant on social and other forums by not using the curse word "crap". As much as I hate it, the cookbook will get a new title no longer being "Cut The Crap Kitchen: How-To Cook On A Budget In Costa Rica". The new title will be "The Ultimate Costa Rica Cookbook: Healthy, Quick & Easy Recipes". This will allow us to be able to continue to sell on the platforms that have been banning us.

We made it another year as I start to get ready to celebrate 22 years of being married to the love of my life. Last year we spent our anniversary on a friend's yacht. Watching the fireworks off the Playa Conchal beaches we were also able to see fireworks clear to Playa Flamingo.

I remember I was scared to death to jump in the pitch-black ocean, but I couldn't resist. No matter how much I begged, Steve would not jump in. Like always Taya came to my rescue holding my hand as we jumped into the obscure ocean. One of the most amazing things I have ever

seen as the abyss illuminates all around me. I was able to check swimming with the photo phytoplankton off my bucket list.

We will be celebrating our anniversary and bringing in the New Year much different tonight. This year I had to cancel our trip to Thailand for our anniversary and Costa Rica has a curfew. To celebrate the end of 2020, we will stay home and have dinner and a movie.

One thing is for sure 2020 has been a roller-coaster of a year. To this day I personally don't know anyone who has passed away from COVID, but I do know that this virus has touched each and every one of around the world in one way or another this year. For us I found it to be a year of growing and learning with an added lesson of what patience is.

Here's to a New Year! 2021 may you bring no masks, good health, happiness, and wealth along with safe international travels.

JANUARY 2021

We Have to Move
January 4, 2021

It's 5:45 am as I hear the truck of workers pull in. The minute there was just a little sunlight at 5:55 am, the first hammer hits the tin, and the saw kicks on. The construction has begun.

Last week I was extremely sad as I packed up the vacation home. Today I'm no longer sad but rather relieved. I am over the moon, excited, and energized with anticipation, along with a big dash of fear and some anxiety.

I'm back to one suitcase, a backpack, and a carry-on just like when we came. Unlike last time, Steve decided to keep the Jeep, packing it with belongings that he is not taking. It's kind of funny to think that my life fits in a jeep and a couple suit cases.

Travel starts in 33 days. I have an airline ticket and no clue where we will end up in the next couple of months. I only know we have a couple of book deadlines and some big goals.

Through this pandemic we have had many discussions on where in the world we want to live. Since we must move anyway, where should we go? We are not quite ready to settle down in our forever home. I am having too much fun experiencing life in different cultures. For our needs and desires we keep coming back to only a few places and Costa Rica is always in the top few.

Steve keeps talking about coming back to Costa Rica and has secured a trip since he chose not to sell the vehicle. But, with all this COVID business I have a strange feeling it's going to be a while before we return.

Beach Sunset
January 8, 2021

It's been way to long…294 days to be exact!

I am so happy beaches are open for sunset. There are more people at tonight's sunset than I have seen in almost a year. Tonight, will be the first time in 294 days since I have seen a beach sunset.

With my butt in the sand and my toes in the water I feel like I'm in heaven. The oranges and yellows burn across the sky with only hints of red. I watch for my favorite part, the green flash. Steve argues with me that it exists, but I swear there is a green flash as the sun kisses the ocean one last time before it drops below the horizon.

There is nothing in the world like beach sunset from the Gold Coast.

Fur Babies Can't Fly
January 11, 2021

It doesn't matter how prepared you are, the rules are changing all the time. We were going to fly our dogs in cargo; however, most airlines are not offering that now. Alaska is the only one flying cargo at this time, but they have 3 layovers so travel time is over 30 hours! That's way too long for my babies! We have our appointments for all the paperwork for emotional support dogs with the doctor and vet next week and our airline tickets have been flagged that we are traveling with animals.

Just our luck, like other airlines, Delta is now not going to allow emotional support animals in the cabin. They are still allowing small ones that fit under the seat but that doesn't help us. It was just a matter of time, but here's the kicker-- I booked our flight with the animals, but all the paperwork must be in by Sunday night and today is late Friday! What are the chances I can pull off getting government stamps done over a weekend plus doctor paperwork?

The Pages did it again, but it took 5 additional calls from Steve to talk to a Delta rep because they had problems getting D.O.G.'s paperwork through! All required paper-work in hand and uploaded. What a mess, but we got it done.

What to Pack
January 15, 2021

Now that we are planning a trip home, I am going to assess what to bring back with me. Time to go room by room to decide what would make our tropical home even better. After packing I have a list of things that were worn out and need replaced. Trips home are always filled with shopping and missing last year's trip put me behind.

We will return with full suitcases of things that are difficult to find or are expensive. If you are planning on making a trip to Costa Rica, we recommend you check out our "Top Travel Items to Pack When Traveling to Costa Rica." You can get my list here:

https://theultimatecostarica.com/228-pack

Tip: We recommend taking your purchased items out of the packaging and remove tags when packing them. It saves space and can save you some money in customs. If the item is in the box or has tags customs may require you to pay tax on it.

We Must Leave
January 19, 2021

Here is the latest update about Costa Rica's visa stamps. According to government reports and media sources they will not be extended past March 2, 2021.

This means that you must leave the country and come back in for a new stamp. Just like before, you don't have to stay out of Costa Rica for any amount of time. You can leave and come right back in; however, at this moment land borders are closed.

As a result, you must do an international flight out and back into the country to receive a new stamp. If you are flying back to the U.S. after January 26, you must show proof of a negative COVID test within three days of travel. And some states have additional requirements.

Keep in mind many other countries, like Canada, are also requiring testing. I called around to many clinics in the Tamarindo area and discovered that the cost is running between $110-$139 per test.

No More Temperature?
January 22, 2021

Prior to 2020, I never thought having my temperature taken would be required to buy a tomato. For almost a year big chain stores that I have shopped at in Costa Rica have taken my temperature before entering. Today none of these stores took my temperature.

Over the months this has just become part of shopping when going to the bigger stores. Even though this has become something that I expect when shopping I still don't feel comfortable. I wish I could tell you why I felt this way. I don't know if this is because a stranger is in my personal space or what. I just know I try to avoid the bigger stores now day.

Weird Day!

January 28, 2021

They did go back to checking temperatures when I went out this week. I wonder what the new requirement will be next week.

Where's the Breaking Point?
January 23, 2021

Snakes

Where do I start with snakes? I don't know about you, but they freak me out. Steve and the kids have always loved them; even having a pet who they named Scales. I never became a fan.

Growing up in Colorado, we were always on the lookout for rattlesnakes, especially when hiking in the mountains. It's not like we didn't know that there were going to be snakes, but nothing could have prepared me for the snakes in Costa Rica.

It did not take long until we saw our first venomous snake. It happened on a trip to a small village named Bijagua. On this particular day, we hiked the path on the finca (farm) that we had been staying at. It was about an hour hike to the top where you could see Lake Nicaragua.

To get to the breathtaking scenery it required a hike through the thick jungle. There was a walking path that the owner had been working on, but the path was narrow and had many leaves and debris on it. Taya had been leading the hike for most of the day. Just writing this brings back the goosebumps! Call it mother intuition or

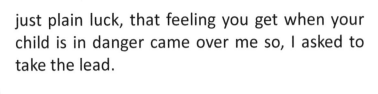

just plain luck, that feeling you get when your child is in danger came over me so, I asked to take the lead.

It was not more than a couple of minutes when I swear to you this little 5-foot woman jumped 10-feet in the air pushing both Steve and Taya backward. Like a wild animal protecting its young while trying not to yell but also scream-ing "snake, snake, snake" continuing to push back as they both were trying to see what had now become the biggest threat of the jungle.

What was an afternoon hike to clear my mind now was a fight for survival! The hill on my right was way too steep to go up but going down was just as steep and if anyone was to slip it would be over! Turning around was not an option at this point. It was late in the afternoon, so the rains had made the trails slicker and more dangerous. As a matter-of-fact, Taya had slipped a couple of times al-ready.

Continuing to push me forwarded their words rang out.

"Woman, there is no snake!"

"Mom come on let me take the lead since you can't see!"

Using the voice that stops my kids in their tracks I whisper shouted,
"SHUT UP & DON'T MOVE!"

All three of us stood like little soldiers at attention, while this crazy mom who could not see pointed out that there was a snake in striking position and having a staring contest less than 3 feet from us.

We were armed with nothing but the walking stick that the owner had said to carry and tap hard on the ground as we walked because the vibrations would help scare off predators like this.

"Steve I almost stepped on it!"

Reminding myself to breathe in through my nose out through the mouth, my fixated eyes widen as I realized the enemy had a triangle-shaped head.

"Woman, you think everything is a snake."

I remind myself this is not a time to agree about who is right or wrong because I'm right, and he's wrong. The snake is about ready to strike at me, not him.

In as calm a voice as I could muster up, the next words came out like a map. He looks like a leaf, the body is curled upright in the middle of that stack of leaves, but his head is sticking up."

"He's poisonous don't move"

I'm corrected quickly as Steve reminds me "the word is venomous, not poisonous".

Snapping quickly back at him "Whatever! The closest hospital is hours away! Get me the hell out of here!"

It's just like him to correct me when facing a life-or-death situation.

Now I don't know about your family, but I can tell you what my family did at this particular moment in time. Cell phones come out while each of them took pictures of what was later confirmed as a Fer de Lance Pit Viper. Basically, it's a jumping Viper and the most dangerous snake in Costa Rica.

After they were done comparing who could get the best picture, we needed to come up with a way out. It was recommended that we use walking sticks, but that had not worked since we had all been doing this when we came into contact. It was clear that the snake had a long body which added to the reach if he were to try to strike. We chose to go down the steep embankment and climb back around on the other side of our predator.

This led to much more of a hike than we anticipated since by that point the rain clouds that we had been trying to outrun for the last hour had caught us. Climbing through the thick brush down a steep incline as the pounding rain hit us. I was caught up in the thick brush. I tried to climb on the other side of our predator while drenched and

watching every step and hand placement because you never know what's hiding.

Stepping onto the path, the clouds had consumed us, and we were no longer able to see what was right in front of us! I felt a sense of peace walking on clouds. It is an amazing feeling, until your child asks, "Now what do we do!". We could not see the path in front of us.

Linking arms, we slowly made it down the rest of the trail that dropped us off at a gate and our cabinas.

I wish I could say this was my only encounter with snakes, but over our years in Costa Rica we have seen dozens of snakes. The biggest was a boa constrictor on our property in Tamarindo. It was about 10-foot-long and Steve made the gardener promise not to kill it. After a couple of pictures, this amazing creature went on its way.

Both dogs have been bitten by snakes in Marbella. Fortunately, we keep meds on hand that the vet had sold us the day we took D.O.G. home from the shelter.

We saw many snakes in Tamarindo but never had any in our homes until Marbella. The first one was the day we moved in and tonight's live snake in the kitchen was about the breaking point for me. We have found multiple snake skins under the furniture that is now moved around weekly. No matter what I do we can't keep them out.

Talk about unwanted house guests!

Thank you, Steve, for relocating him.

Testing to go Home, Visa is Up
January 27, 2021

Heads up U.S. friends, Costa Rica immigration just confirmed it will no longer be extending tourist visas. Everyone who has been in the country on an extended visa due to the pandemic must leave on or before March 2, 2020, this includes me and my family.

I sat back and watched last week as the new United States President Biden signed an executive order right after being sworn in on January 20th changing travel laws. Now travelers will be required to get negative Covid test to travel. It's like a no win either way you cut it as people from the U.S. cancel international travel because of the extra cost and hassle. It's now going to cost at least an extra $260 to travel home. This extra expense is why you always have a backup account with some extra funds when traveling.

Some may say testing is a small price to pay to travel during a pandemic while other would question the legal rights that a citizens would have when traveling back to their home country. The part that leaves me scratching my head is how President Biden is only mandating that the airlines require test but not land borders.

One of my questions is why is it easier for illegal immigrants to get into the U.S. than the people who are cit-

izens? Today I watch and read the news about the crisis of the undocumented people coming over the Mexico border into the U.S. I find myself appalled at what is going on. Undocumented people are being allowed over the Mexico border into Texas without paperwork, COVID-19 testing, and quarantining.

Watching the news reports of dozens of people who are not masked or tested being taken from the border on bus to hotels and gyms, is not only alarming but once again makes me question everything that is going on. How is it that all these migrants are coming in without testing and not masking while testing and masking is being forced on American citizens who are returning to their home country?

One thing is for sure, Costa Rica never required their citizen to test when coming back home. However, Other counties like Canada have not only kept borders tightly closed they also have mandated testing for their citizens to return home.

Added to this I have heard horror stories from some travelers who have been placed in government camps and hotels upon return. They were told this was for quarantine and testing purpose. The people who I have talked to say they were locked in a room alone for days and sometimes even weeks. They were not allowed outside food and what was served was awful. Some people even reported not being allowed contact through Internet with others.

Let's face it, I'm not the one who is choosing to travel right now, Costa Rica is not extending my visa. That means I must leave the country and should be going back to my home country. As much as this chica is home sick, I would have put travel off for 90 more days if my visa had been extended.

Reaching out to multiple agencies to this day I have still not received clarification as to why Costa Rica dropped testing to come in. Once thing is for sure the U.S. has sent aid to Costa Rica in the form of COVID tests.

Words from two of my conspiracy theory children were much the same as they pleaded "mom, please don't let them stick that swab up your noise!" Their concerns are that some tests in the beginning had been found to be contaminated. As I go back to reread the old news reports and videos they had sent me last year, I find all of the articles and videos have been pulled down.

My children have begged me to not test and find a county that is currently not testing to travel to. This would allow me to fly out and back into Costa Rica where I would receive a new 90-day visa stamp and no swab.

What I do find is reports showing it was false information, as the CDC also makes a lot of excuses as to why a test could become contaminated.

My government has presumed me and others to be sick not allowing us to come back to our home county until we prove we are healthy. I guess the undocumented must be immune to this virus since many are being allowed in without any testing.

I feel my rights as a U.S. citizen are being violated since I'm not allowed back in without EXPENSIVE testing and paperwork while other who are not citizens are being let in without these requirements.

Since my government is requiring the test and our insurance at this time does not cover testing outside of the U.S. this will be an out-of-pocket expense. Now I will pay to have a test that I'm 99% sure came from my country as aid to Costa Rica in order to return stateside.

The more I think about this the fishier it sounds. I hate to say it, we will all just have to sit back and see if Steve and I get sick in the next six to eight months like my kids are predicting.

FEBRUARY 2021

Place Your Bets
February 1, 2021

How many times does it take Steve and Nikki to get a Riteve 2021 vehicle inspection sticker? We passed last year our first time around. It was an interesting adventure watching Steve use his Spanish while they told him to do things in words that he had never heard before. It doesn't help that the man can't hear and the garage you drive through is loud making the whole thing seem even funnier.

Last year Steve just showed up. He tried to make an appointment but when it asked him for his Cédula number (like a social security number) he was unaware that he could put in his passport number. This year an appointment is a must.

I think we would have passed if the water truck had not hit us in the gas station parking lot. Right then and there we should have just turned around, but nope! After a quick inspection, everything looks good. The truck just rubbed the tire that was turned out, but boy did it shake the jeep.

The inspection was going great, right until they ask Steve to turn the blinkers on. Are you kidding me? We just had this problem fixed by the mechanics last week and they even worked when we pulled in.

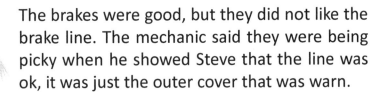

The brakes were good, but they did not like the brake line. The mechanic said they were being picky when he showed Steve that the line was ok, it was just the outer cover that was warn.

We don't know any of the mechanics in the area, so I took my friends advice and we drove to her mechanic in Santa Cruz about 20 minutes away.

After grabbing a bite and killing a couple hours we were back on the road to see if we can get re-inspected today. We are running out of days to get the inspection done before our flight.

We made it back to the inspection and they were able to fit us into their schedule without an appointment. This was after a three hour wait in the sun.

On the second time at what I like to call the video game part, they have the wheels spin, then they tell you to brake, and you can watch the red light turn green. We had no problem with this part last time, it should turn green at any moment. Nothing like having work done, then fail because the brakes had not been bled right.

Now the other guy doesn't like the light bar that's on top of the Beast. After 5 years we were told that they had to come down. Over the years we have known this could be flagged but turning them to face inside has always been sufficient. Not today.

No Riteve sticker today, I guess we'll hope the third time is the charm.

February 3, 2021

Now to try a 3rd time. Not again, the blinkers are giving us trouble again! We checked them before we left and again when we pulled in. Steve, had every worker in the whole garage laughing at the crazy gringo man who had jumped out of the Jeep, running around, and banging on the breaker box. I jumped over the console so I could mess with the steering column until they started again.

At that moment I don't think any of them had the heart to not give us a sticker. One thing was for sure, they all were very aware that Steve was not going to pay anyone to run it through. It did not matter how many times they sent him away, he had accepted their challenge.

If you have ever been through this process, you know that it can be nail-biting as you watch them stand at the computer not knowing if you are going to get a passing sticker or a failed paper. There it is that beautiful sticker! Watching him fist bump my husband as we all celebrate what Steve and I now referred to as our Costa Rica "Amazing Race". If you have never seen this reality show, I highly recommend checking it out. The game show contestants travel the world while having crazy obstacles and challenges thrown at them.

Our obstacle now is that Riteve has cut into our moving days. I only have one more day to get everything to the consignment store and pick the stamped government paperwork up for the dogs to travel since tomorrow is a no-drive day. Can't forget COVID testing in there as well - nothing like cutting it right to the very end.

Our Last Night
February 05, 2021

If you are liquidating, there's an amazing consignment store in Villa Real. "The Consignment Store" is located at Centro Commercial Royal Palms, next to Mega Súper. Jacqueline, the owner, is great! We just took truckloads to her, and she did a full inventory and priced it out and took her split.

The payment was sent to us via PayPal and what does not sell we will have her donate. Wish there had been a store like this when we moved here. They have things from all over the world. It will be one of my first stops in the future after we see what the next house needs.

We did it! The packed Jeep is stored, and housekeepers are showing up after we leave. There is nothing more to do but wait for our COVID test results that are now 45 minutes late and no one is picking up the phone. After a couple of hours and many calls, they finally pick up and say they will resend them. It only took a couple of minutes and we both are dancing around the room at the negative tests. The dogs have their stamped paperwork, we have our paperwork and now we pray there are no roadblocks or car problems tomorrow.

This CHICA is coming home! It's been 19 months since I have set foot on U.S. soil. My country has a new leader, and the world has started to get vaccinated. The fighting continues over masks and how safe the vaccines are. It's going to be interesting to see what this new world looks like, but one thing is for sure, I can't wait to see everyone.

Traveling Stateside
February 06, 2021

Well, here we go today we are going stateside. We drink our last cup of morning coffee as we let the dogs run the Marbella beach before loading up and head to Liberia. I find myself blessed as I walk the beach with the love of my life, and one of our dearest friends Stacey who has been here for over 25 years.

I ask myself if the pandemic won or if this is just another season? Like so many other expat friends she will be moving her family back to the U.S. next month. Our intentions are to come back to Costa Rica, but we have no return date and with the state of the world this chica has a strange feeling it's going to be a while.

One thing is for sure, I'm more scared about flying these dogs than I was with my kids when they were little. Like I said before, we have been working with and training them for this day. But here is the catch, no matter how much we work trying to prepare D.O.G. and Titan, being in an airport and on a plane is nothing that I can truly simulate at home. In addition, the world is masked and we have been trying to avoid people.

Pulling up to the Liberia airport it looks much the same except the one washing station that has been placed outside the front entrance. Here goes nothing as the dog's leashes are linked to their harnesses and suitcase are unloaded.

I am struggling to wash my hands with the suitcase and D.O.G. who is behaving but looking around like it's party time as a couple other dogs walk by. Breathe chica, the day is going to be long and full of people and obviously other canines.

The Liberia airport is small with only two stories and all the airline counters are in one little section. Masked, armed with paperwork and passports, we're shuffled through our first body scanner. Neither of us have temperatures and we are allowed into the next step of the airport.

Heading through the Delta line, our passports are checked just like before. The next person checks our COVID tests from off Steve's cell phone confirming they were nega-

tive. We had to sign another form about masking travel and our covid testing. I had read all these forms before we got to the airport to make sure I knew what I was signing.

Next step was the ticket counter. This girl can pack as both suitcases weighed exactly 50lbs. After checking in and some copies of the dog's paperwork the only thing left was security. This was pretty uneventful as there was only a couple other people and they gave the dogs treats.

The seating in the upper terminal had every other seat blocked out. As we waited to board the flight, I notice that the plane is out on the tarmac. This is about the time Steve said they are going to make us walk down the stairs and out to the aircraft and back up another flight of stairs. I have done this many times before but never at this airport. What would the odds be that I would have to haul a backpack and extremely heavy carry-on making my way down two flights of metal steps with a leashed dog and then expect him to walk up the next metal stairway into that big plane?

Once again, no matter how much training we did nothing could have compared to the real thing. They called people for early boarding and the plane was still sitting across the tarmac. It took a little nudging, but we did it down and up the steps, even down the little aisle of the aircraft.

Let's face it there is never enough room when flying unless the flight is almost empty. As people file in, a couple families sit in groups but for the most part this leg of the trip is empty, allowing Steve and me to both have our own row of seats.

About the time the wheels started to come off the ground I found myself holding a 59lb black lab in my lap as D.O.G. jumped up. Reassuring him that he was ok after a couple minutes both dogs and us settled in for the intentional flight to Atlanta George (ATL).

There is nothing like being 30,000 feet in the air, from the smell of jet fuel and the recycled air. The pilot comes over the intercom announcing the seatbelt light has been turned off. It was as if I had been shocked back to life. All of this travel leaves me feeling like I'm human again.

Let's face it this chica was born to travel. There is no drink service, but the flight attends passed out a plastic bag with a couple small bottles of water and two bags of cracker snacks. Now don't get me wrong, D.O.G. also got a treat but nothing like his little brother Titan as the flight attendant flirted with Steve stopping and giving his puppy extra treats over the next few hours.

Landing was easy, it took about thirty minutes to get through customs. We were pushed through the line because of the animals. Picking up a quick snack and board-

ing the final flight, I find a strange peace about being back on U.S. soil. The seating was also marked off for social distancing just like the Costa Rica airport. For the most part people who were not eating had their mask on.

The next leg of the flight was much like the first, a few more people but everyone who wanted a full row of seats got one. D.O.G. handles take off much better this time. Drinks and snacks were the same as on the first leg. This chica is missing her drink service during the flight.

Landing in cold Colorado, I could feel the crisp cold air as I step off the flight. Walking through the terminal it looked much like it would around midnight. Only a couple of terminals where people are about ready to board red-eye flights.

The one thing that stood out was there was no social distancing from the seating to standing. Maybe this is because they know they are going to pack all these people on a flight and then make them stand side by side in custom lines.

Home, the word is indescribable. Gathering our bags, we walked out to be greeted by my father-in-law and our son. I have not seen either of these men since they dropped me off at the airport over a year and a half ago. One thing is for sure a year and a half is too long to be

away from my kids and family. This momma is over the moon with excitement.

Even though quarantine is not mandated its recommended by the CDC. However, nothing was said throughout our whole trip. I now will say goodbye to my husband and son again as we go into quarantine. Steve will return with his dad and our son to quarantine as I go to my dad's where I will quarantine. Ten days until we can see the rest of our family.

Isolation

What can I say, isolation and lock-down sucks. So close yet so far away, my family is just down the street. One of the things that many people don't know is that my mom became very ill after the first part of the year. Receiving a call that my mom has now lost almost all her vision I count the days hours and even minutes until I can come out of quarantine and see her.

Over the next fourteen days I spend a lot of time writing and soul searching. What can I say, being locked away with your thoughts can be dangerous or therapeutic depending on how you use the time. I'm hoping to come out of this time a better person while also accomplishing a list of tasks that I must work on.

Once thing is for sure, I have a lot to reflect on and days to do it.

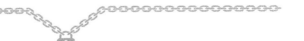

MARCH 2021

Losing Bets
March 2, 2021

If I had placed my bets, this woman would have lost. Wow, I wish I could say I was shocked, but after this last year I'm starting to think nothing should shock me anymore. If you have been staying on an extended tourist visa due to the pandemic, today is the last day to leave Costa Rica.

Let's face, it there are a handful of people that have flights out today, but the majority of people who have not left were never planning to in the first place. I have heard all the excuses in the travel groups from people being scared (I'm not trying to downplay their fears) to travelers who are just using the pandemic as an excuse to break the rules.

Anyway you cut it, the government felt it was safe enough for all the people here to travel. They have been telling us multiple times over the last two months there is no way they were going to extend visas. Now the Costa Rica government is not stupid. They were aware that many of the expats and vacationers here would just catch a flight out and right back.

This tells me the country felt safe enough for people to leave and come back in. Remember they will have the added insurance that will cover some bills if they get

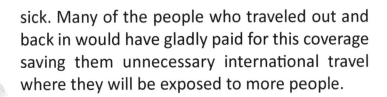

sick. Many of the people who traveled out and back in would have gladly paid for this coverage saving them unnecessary international travel where they will be exposed to more people.

Most of the people who I have talked to traveled to countries that did not require testing. Now that masses have traveled out and back in. I want to take a minute to say congratulation to the tourists who put off travel to the last minute, or had no plans of leaving.

Nothing like the government changing their mind at the last moment allowing the people who did not leave to stay an additional 90 days.

JUNE 2021

That Feeling
June 4, 2021

Published author of two best sellers here and I still have a hard time putting the feeling into words, especially this time. Maybe bitter-sweet would be the words to describe what came over me after watching another book that has been in the works for years start its final journey before it hits the reader's hands. This is the sweet part. Now here's the bitter part, Steve beat me to publishing. If I could put an angry emoji here I would!

Don't get me wrong, this wife is so proud of her husband, but for those of you who don't know, there has been a little battle going on in the Page household the last year.

The Fruits of COVID

Both of us have been writing like crazy authors together, however, when the craziness started it became very apparent that my marriage was not going to make it through lock-down if we did not have some separation.

Yep, you all know what I'm talking about now. If I had written this 15 months ago, most of the world had no clue how hard it is to spend 24 hours a day with your

spouse and children. These are the challenges of working from home that many people are just now getting to experience.

For me, this has been the life since we moved 5 years ago. It took almost a year for us to get a routine down with growing pains that left us wanting to give up most days, but let me tell you when the Page household finally got it down it was like a working piece of well-oiled machinery.

Life threw a wrench in my perfect world as we went into tighter lock-down. The chica that never left the porch found herself wanting to run away again while she watched her husband start to lose his joy in their everyday life. How could this be? We had lived away from the world for so long so why was it so hard?

To answer this question, we need to look at the bigger picture. Steve and I have owned and operated many corporations over the decades making us no strangers to how hard this kind of work can be on a couple. The move to Costa Rica was scary as hell for us and having to work together on a whole new level proved to be stimulating.

It was like adding fuel to a spark that I thought was once lost, igniting burning fire to our marriage and reuniting us on a whole new level. It was about survival. We had to rely on each other because little things like paying a water bill or even ordering a pizza had become an adventure.

But let's face it that was 5 years ago and both of us could do this stuff blindfolded now.

Before COVID, Steve was volunteering at the church, giving me my alone time. My shopping trips or when one of us walked the beach alone would give us at least moments apart, none of this is happening now. My women's trips and his men's prayer retreats or whatever they do when they all take off for a week have been non-existent.

Let's face it. No humans, including spouses, are designed to be with each other 24 hours a day 7 days a week. They become like rats in a cage. So, what do you do when the country takes away your driving privileges, locks you in zones while closing down the country? You kick your husband that has been a Debbie downer to the other cabina to work on his own project. This proved to backfire for me as it gave him time to focus more, and he gained the edge. Apparently, I am not as efficient on my own.

Even when we returned, we spent time individually since he chose to stay with his parents and I with mine during the quarantine time.

We have been back to working together for a while now even though we have been focusing on separate books for quite some time. Let me be the first to say Congratulation to Steve on your first action fiction book "Drifting Smoke", is now published on Kindle Vella during their

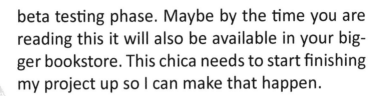

beta testing phase. Maybe by the time you are reading this it will also be available in your bigger bookstore. This chica needs to start finishing my project up so I can make that happen.

Tip: Never tell your opponent your deadline. Over the months it has become a battle to see who would publish first and today he won.

JULY 2021

Missing My Sunsets, but I'm Not Alone.
July 7, 2021

I'm now watching Costa Rica lock-down from afar. It's sad because although the beaches were opened during the day, they closed again during sunset hours in May 2021. This was due to a spike in the numbers and full hospital beds. As of today, July 22, 2021, they are open, even though the number are still rising.

One of the questions I ask is how hard will it be to find beach views in 2022. I have been looking and found a couple one bedroom and studios for around $700 - $800 that are ocean front. I have lived very close to the beach but never ocean front, that would be a dream come true. I still don't know if I would do it without hot water though.

Passport Warning
July 22, 2021

I learn something new every day.

If you are planning on traveling internationally in the next year, get your passport now!!!

It's has been taking months to get passports. I know people who have been waiting over 12 weeks.

The rules to board most international fights say you need at least 6 months left on your passport. If 2020 showed us anything, it's that lock-down can happen quickly, and the airlines were thinking ahead. Trust me, it sucks to have an expired passport in a country that is locked down. Your embassy has limited staff, or even closed for months creating more of a problem for tourists and expats.

Here's what I learned today. If you are waiting on a passport and have travel coming up, you can contact your congressmen and tell them the problem. They have the ability to rush your passport through.

I was just in a travel group that was debating this topic. Some will tell you that this should only be used if there is an emergency. These same people said these people have better things to do than to make sure you can go on

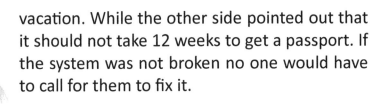

vacation. While the other side pointed out that it should not take 12 weeks to get a passport. If the system was not broken no one would have to call for them to fix it.

This is me speaking to you as a travel writer. Yes, the system is broken, however even before the world went to crap it took planning and paper-work. Consider yourself warned. I have seen people turned away at the airport counter for not having enough time and can tell you dozens of stories about canceled trips because people did not take the time to do their paperwork and overnight is not an option in most states right now.

The world is opening back up, are you ready to book your international travels? Now that the U.S. Embassy in Costa Rica has re-opened, it is taking about 3 weeks to process a U.S. passport renewal.

Last Entry
July 23, 2021

I write this entry from my dad's farmhouse in Colorado. I can officially say that the last 30 days have been some of the hardest in my life. Last month my son was in a horrific motorcycle crash that almost killed him. That was just the beginning.

After the accident we had all made sure to wear masks everywhere to avoid bringing contagions into the hospital. The only places we went were the hospital, the grocery store, and home to sleep. We maintained social distancing and were careful to sanitize. We could not afford to make our son sick while trying to heal from his injuries.

Two and a half weeks later, while he laid in the CICU on life support machines, Steve tested positive for COVID at which time we were told that he had to stay out of the hospital and quarantine for 10 days and at least 24 hours with no fever.

Since my test was negative, I am required to spend 14 days out of the hospital from the day I separated from my husband. I wasn't required to quarantine, but I was not able to visit my husband or enter the hospital. They said it was because I could develop COVID from being exposed to Steve. Should my employer require one, they told me

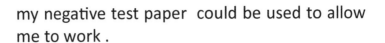

my negative test paper could be used to allow me to work .

It doesn't make sense that none of the nurses or doctors that had been around Steve, even the ones who had not been vaccinated, were not sent home. I guess their masks have special powers when they put them on. I was only potentially contagious to those in the hospital who were not working, whatever.

Let me tell you, COVID is nothing to mess with! Steve went on to be sick for 20 days running a 105ºF temp while isolating and taking care of himself. He told me the pain was excruciating. I have never felt so helpless as a wife or mother.

After seeing how sick Steve became and because I am immune deficient, we decided it was best for me to get the vaccine. I am not fully at peace with this decision because I don't believe the proper case studies have been done. Don't get me wrong, I believe that most vaccines are necessary. But the COVID vaccinations seem too rushed for me to be comfortable at this time.

The only reason I did it is because my husband said he thinks if I get COVID with my health conditions it would kill me. But at this moment the shot also has potential to do the same thing. I guess we will all sit back and see what happens over the next decade. Upside, I can now travel international since most countries are requiring a vaccine to enter. Getting vaccinated was going to happen

sometime, but I really did want to wait for a couple years and was even willing to give up travel.

After spending 16 days away from my husband and being allowed back in the hospital for two days, I tested positive for COVID.

We were told it had been too long and Steve was most likely not who had infected me. Maybe it's because I was partially vaccinated. I'd had 1 vaccination and a rapid test. I was told this could be a false positive and I could retest with a 72-hour test. To me it did not matter because I was told I had to isolate either way. Once again, I locked myself away from the world and my husband.

The last 14 days have been not much more than a bad cold thank GOD. I have never been so thankful to be Stateside. I can't wait for tomorrow when Steve (who is now healthy) and Ellis (who is just gotten out of the hospital after 37 days) join me. Ellis will need help with the months of therapy that are awaiting him.

Being locked down in a foreign country to come home to parents that had aged even more than I could have imagined was hard. But that combined with almost losing a child again have all been very life-altering. Life is short and can change in a split second.

Embrace the Good, the Bad, and the Ugly. I might be a little scared to get on an international flight right now, but I'm very aware of how cold Colorado gets during winter. You never know where this chica and her backpack will end up.

Safe Travels in the new world!

THE END!

AUGUST 2021

Latest Travel Requirements
August 1, 2021

Costa Rica is open and those who have been vaccinated can come without insurance as of August 1, 2021. For the most part, the country is back to normal. Last I checked masks were still required, unlike Colorado where barely anyone is masking nowadays. Don't forget the driving restrictions are still crazy and changing all the time.

If you are traveling to the airport, the restrictions don't apply, but you or your driver will need to have proof of the itinerary. I don't see this changing anytime soon since Costa Rica is bragging about how auto accident deaths are down. If you rent a car, the daytime restrictions don't apply but the nighttime ones do.

Don't forget your onward travel. Remember, the number of days on your visa is all up to customs officers. If you have your paperwork, there is less likelihood of having problems.

The onward travel QR code/health pass is still required to be completed even if you are vaccinated. If you are not vaccinated, make sure you get COVID insurance that meets the requirement and make sure it's the same day as your onward travel. I recommend insurance more than ever now, even if vaccinated.

At this time, the U.S. is requiring testing to go home unless you can prove a positive followed by a negative test in the last 90 days. I guess this is an upside to being sick. We get to save a little time and money on our return trip if we go in the next 90 days.

You can get tested at the airport if you have a later flight, but if your flight is early, there will not be enough time. However, there are places throughout the country to get tested. The average test is $60-$120 or roughly 33,0000- 66,0000 colones. Some of my friends have told me they used home testing kits they brought from the U.S., and they were accepted.

For the most updated rules and laws, check with your embassy.

Scan Me

Check out More!

For a complete list of my books including new releases, please visit my author page:

www.vivapurpose.com/nikki-page/

You may enjoy some of our content on our websites:

www.theultimatecostarica.com
www.cutthecrapcostarica.com
www.vivapurpose.com

Nikki Page
#1 International Best Selling Author

WORKS CITED

A.M. Costa Rica. Country Opens First Hospital for Only Attending Covid-19 Patients, 11 Mar. 2020, amcostarica.com/Country%20opens%20first%20hospital%20for%20only%20attending%20covid-19%20patients.html.

ACSSANJOE, . "Health Alert – U.S. Embassy San Jose, 25 Mar. 2020.

ACSSANJOSE. Travel Alert: Global Level 4 Health Advisory, 19 Mar. 2020.

Alvarado, Sebastian, et al. "Important: Foreign Nationals Who Leave Costa Rica during the Covid-19 Crisis Will Lose Their Status." Outlier Legal Services, 2 Oct. 2020, news.outlierlegal.com/2020/03/23/important-foreign-nationals-leaves-costa-rica-during-the-covid-19-crisis-will-lose-their-status/.

Breastcancer.org, . "Exposure to Chemicals in Plastic." Breastcancer.org, 11 Sept. 2020, www.breastcancer.org/risk/factors/plastic.

Chavez, Nicole, and Dakin Andone. "CDC Recommends Americans Wear Face Masks Voluntarily in Public but Some Officials Say They Felt 'Pressured' to Draft New Guidelines." CNN, Cable News Network, 4 Apr. 2020, www.cnn.com/2020/04/03/health/us-coronavirus-friday/index.html.

Ellis, Ralph. "Who Changes Stance, Says Public Should Wear Masks." WebMD, WebMD, 8 June 2020, www.webmd.com/lung/news/20200608/who-changes-stance-says-public-should-wear-masks.

Esquivel, Por Noelia. "Cinco Municipalidades De GUANACASTE Aprueban Ley Seca Por Emergencia Del Covid-19." Voz De Guanacaste, 20 Apr. 2020, vozdeguanacaste.com/cinco-municipalidades-de-guanacaste-aprueban-ley-seca-por-emergencia-del-covid-19/.

Gelder, Koen van. "Price per Unit HOUSEHOLD Paper PRODUCTS U.S. 2020." Statista, 15 Jan. 2021, www.statista.com/statistics/1088524/price-per-unit-of-household-paper-products/.

Harris, William, et al. "Urgent Information Regarding Residencies & Tourist Status." Outlier Legal Services, 2 Oct. 2020, news.outlierlegal.com/2020/03/17/urgent-information-regarding-residencies-and-tourist-sta-

tus/?fbclid=IwAR3U-1H8suoX-OTWNE9esnOOjhC7z1K75jl3ry-Qn-8D103L3zERqi0X1EBU.

Ianzito, Christina. "Harvard Study Says Flying During Pandemic Is Low-Risk." AARP, 29 Oct. 2020, www.aarp.org/travel/travel-tips/safety/info-2020/harvard-study-on-covid-19-flying-risk.html.

Johncox, Cassidy. "COVID-19 in the Us: TRACKING States with the Most Cases, Deaths on Aug. 25." WDIV, WDIV ClickOnDetroit, 25 Aug. 2020, www.clickondetroit.com/news/national/2020/08/25/covid-19-in-the-us-tracking-states-with-the-most-cases-deaths-on-aug-25/.

Morris, John. "American Airlines Policy Effectively Bans Power Wheelchair Users from Flying to 130 U.S. Airports." Wheelchair Travel, 28 Oct. 2020, wheelchairtravel.org/american-airlines-policy-prohibits-power-wheelchairs-regional-jets/.

Page, Nicole, et al. "The Day a Bird Named 'Captain Crunch' Came into Our Lives." The Howler Magazine, 25 Mar. 2021, howlermag.com/the-day-a-bird-named-captain-crunch-came-into-our-lives/.

Page, Steve. "Costa Rica Tropical Storms: What You Need to Know ABOUT Rainy Season." Cut the Crap Costa Rica, 30 Aug. 2021, cutthecrapcostarica.com/costa-rica-tropical-storms/.

Ramirezej | 9 April, 2020 | Topics: Alert. "Travel Alert: U.S. Embassy San Jose (9 April 2020)." U.S. Embassy in Costa Rica, 9 Apr. 2020, cr.usembassy.gov/200409-travel-alert/.

Thomas, Pete. "Officer Appears to Shoot Gun While Chasing Surfer on Closed Beach." USA Today, Gannett Satellite Information Network, 30 Mar. 2020, ftw.usatoday.com/2020/03/officer-shoots-gun-while-chasing-surfer-on-closed-beach.

The Tico Times, . "Costa Rica Overwhelmed by Coronavirus Testing as Panama Records First Death: What You Need to Know Today." The Tico Times | Costa Rica News | Travel | Real Estate, 11 Mar. 2020, ticotimes.net/2020/03/11/costa-rica-overwhelmed-by-coronavirus-testing-as-panama-records-first-death-what-you-need-to-know-today.

Times, The Tico, et al. "News Briefs: President Alvarado Investigated after Taking Vacation." The Tico Times | Costa Rica News | Travel | Real Estate, 12 Aug. 2020, ticotimes.net/2020/08/12/news-briefs-president-alvarado-investigated-after-taking-vacation.

Wong, Wilson. "Chicago Mayor Lori Lightfoot Defends Hairstylist Visit amid Coronavirus Outbreak." NBCNews.com, NBCUniversal News Group, 11 Apr. 2020, www.nbcnews.com/news/nbcblk/chicago-mayor-defends-hairstylist-visit-amid-coronavirus-outbreak-n1181546.

Zúñiga, Alejandro. "Costa Rica up to 177 KNOWN Coronavirus Cases; New Driving Restrictions BEGIN Tonight." The Tico Times | Costa Rica News | Travel | Real Estate, 24 Mar. 2020, ticotimes.net/2020/03/24/costa-rica-up-to-177-known-coronavirus-cases-new-driving-restrictions-begin-tonight.